THE
HUMAN BODY
Owners Workshop Manual

Second Edition

Allegedly K. A. Dave

Models covered

Human Male, Human Female, Couch potato and all Sporty models

Does not cover Pleiadians, Extra Terrestrial Humanoids or the French.

Allegedly Books

While this book is written in a somewhat light-hearted manner, the information and therapies presented in this book are factually correct, life changing and potentially lifesaving.

ISBN 978-1-291-99119-2

For Sylvia, with my eternal gratitude.

Acknowledgements

I would like to give a great big thank you to Veronika Valovics, my Impossible Girl, for putting up with hearing me repeating the same "bullshit" over and over again before I finally got around to writing it all down, and for encouraging me to continue writing whenever I got distracted by bright shiny objects.

I am eternally grateful to Sylvia Chandler, the amazing woman who first started me on the path to near perfect health, as well as Andy Relf, my soul brother, who not only came along with me to Sylvia's presentation but has also taken this incredible journey in parallel with my own.

Thanks also to Bob Hodgson for his support and enthusiasm during the early stages of writing; I'm not sure how far along I'd have been without it.

I am grateful to Liam Pritchard for volunteering his time and energy to proof-read this book. Thanks Liam, it couldn't have been easy :D.

Thanks too, to Sandie Darling and Andy Williamson - whose friendship, hospitality, bullying, counselling, and copious amounts of nasty chocolate contributed greatly to my peace of mind and the completion of this book

I would like to express my appreciation to all the members of "The Distillery" Facebook group - you guys are amazing and beautiful people, your journeys are an inspiration to all and I am honoured to be counted among your number.

I want to also thank the universal super-beings, Jade and Connor for continuously teaching me life lessons while cunningly pretending to be small children.

Finally, I'd like to thank my Mum for her lifelong support and for the magical bond we share that can only be formed when a mother and son sit and watch Star Trek together.

Disclaimer

Note to those seeking medical advice

Nothing in this book is to be construed as medical advice.

Allegedly Dave has legible handwriting and does not play golf. He has neither a white coat nor a fancy certificate on the wall; he is not a doctor, nor does he have any desire to be one.

None of the healing modalities detailed within are medicinal in any way shape or form, rather they are time honoured, tried and tested therapies and practices that rely on allowing and assisting the body to heal itself and have existed for thousands of years before the establishment of the current allopathic medical system.

As these natural therapies are decidedly not medicinal, it cannot be claimed that Allegedly Dave is "practicing medicine" without a licence. There is no practicing involved whatsoever.

If, however, you are seeking medical advice or treatment then by all means take your chances with a doctor, who would undoubtedly be as pleased as punch to write out a prescription for some noxious pharmaceutical that **will** fund his next golfing trip to the Bahamas and might make your symptoms go away... for a while.

Note to offended Doctors

I make no apologies for the language I employ when I refer to you., I'm sure most of you have the health and wellbeing of your patients uppermost in your heart and not all of you are in it for the money, social status and free golf bags, but it cannot have escaped your notice that your surgeries are increasingly packed with sicker and sicker individuals; the number of diseases, maladies and disorders are increasing faster than the medical reference books can list them; and strangely enough, a pharmaceutical treatment is usually already on the market to treat them.

It should be obvious to even the most overworked GP that the allopathic method of treating only the symptoms of an illness with no regard to the cause simply **DOES NOT WORK!** (Unless, of course, it is the GP's intention to just "treat" the patients in such a way as to keep them as lifelong customers rather than heal them - in which case it works just fine.)

It should be equally obvious that behind this slow poisoning of the population is a massive corporate machine that has a voracious appetite for the trillions of dollars it devours each year.

Table of Contents

"The worst thing is watching someone drown and not being able to convince them that they can save themselves by just standing up." – Anon.

Introduction

About Your Human Body

The human body first appeared in its current form around 350,000 years ago, though many archaeologists believe it has been around a lot longer. While some consider the human body is a product of Darwinian Evolution, no evidence has, as yet, surfaced to support this view. There does, however, appear to be a great deal of circumstantial evidence to support the supposition that the modern human body was created or genetically altered from an existing species of hominid by an external agency.

The human body is offered in two body plans, Male and Female, so that users can experience different and exciting levels of fun, hilarity, moodiness and self loathing. It also comes in all shapes and sizes and is available in most colours except Green, Indigo or Violet.

Various shades of blue have also been offered, but they proved unpopular with customers.

Colloidal Silver Blue – Healthy, but not a popular look.

Shiny Bald Guy Blue – Very, very cool, but still, no thanks!

Living With Your Human Body

The idea of having a manual for your body might seem rather redundant to most but consider this: When we arrive in the world, we essentially figure out how to do things by ourselves.

Of course our parents teach us to stand and take our first steps, but it is we who teach ourselves how to walk and we consequently develop our own unique gait and stride mostly by trial, error and accident. We may not develop a particularly efficient style of locomotion - it may even be one injurious to our health. But for better or worse, this then becomes the way we walk. And barring injury, we rarely change once the pattern becomes ingrained, and it is rarer still that we make the connection with back problems, in our later years, to practices we taught ourselves in our earliest.

In the world today, approximately 66 million people die every year. Of that: Approximately 17 million people die of Cardiovascular disease; 10 million succumb to Cancer; 3.3 million die of AIDS; and 180,000 people die from Diabetes. In some third world countries infectious diseases are as epidemic as Obesity and Asthma are in the developed nations.

The human body is not as badly designed as we are being led to believe. It is an amazing, intelligent, self-repairing community which, without external interference, will completely regenerate and renew itself just about every seven years.

Despite a staggering figure of 36 million people who apparently die of something called "old age" every year, the eminent physiologists and doctors of the last century conceded that there is no such thing as chronological aging:

Dr. John Gardner, in his book "Longevity" wrote,

> "It is more difficult, on scientific grounds, to explain why man dies at all, than it is to believe in the duration of human life for a thousand years."

Dr. William Hammond in his book, "How to Live Forever", wrote:

> "There is no physiological reason known at the present day why man should die."

Dr. James T. Monroe said:

> "The human frame as a machine is perfect. It contains within itself no marks by which we can possibly predict its decay. It is apparently intended to go on forever."

Dr. George W. Crile concluded:

> "There is no natural death. All deaths from so-called natural causes are merely the end-products of a progressive acid saturation"

Dr. Emphringham declares:

> "All creatures automatically poison themselves, not TIME, but these toxic products produce the senile changes that we call old age."

Dr. Alexis Carrel, in his classic book "Man, The Unknown", asserted:

> "The cell is immortal. It is merely the fluid in which it floats that degenerates. Renew this fluid at proper intervals, and give the cell proper nourishment upon which to feed, and, so far as we know, the pulsation of life may go on forever."

Nobody actually dies of old age; With the exception of terminal trauma, everyone dies of some pre-existing condition resulting from accumulated toxins and toxic thought patterns. Sometimes this toxicity is forced upon us by our immediate environment. Sometimes they are a result of an accident. Sometimes we adopt toxic habits.

For many people, the process of 'learning to live' doesn't go much further than the day to day routines of the modern lifestyle, the responsibility for our health is delegated to experts because of a belief that such experts know more about our bodies than we do.

Equipped with this book, you will learn three invaluable skills:

- Reading the body's warning indicators
- Responding correctly to warnings
- Reprogramming the body

When good maintenance is added to these skills then your human body will remain in excellent condition far beyond its "expected" lifetime.

Reading the body's warning indicators

The modern medical establishment calls these warning indicators *"symptoms"* and misinterprets them as *"the problem to treat"* rather than an alert that the body is dealing with a particular issue, thus the modern allopathic approach is like a mechanic **removing the bulb** from a car's Oil Warning indicator, which is lit because a leak has reduced the oil levels. The indicator is no longer lit and so the symptom is considered treated, however, the leak continues and the engine will eventually seize (which the allopathic mechanic will convince you is a totally separate and unrelated matter.)

Responding correctly to warnings

In this western culture we have lost the ability to understand the language that our bodies use to communicate with us, and we have subsequently received an alternate interpretation of their meaning, which is usually the complete opposite of what they actually mean.

If we learn to respond correctly to the messages that the body is sending, our actions will no longer hinder our body's efforts to heal itself, the warning indications will vanish, and we will have improved our understanding of ourselves and thus the quality of our lives going forward.

Reprogramming the body

The human body is in some respects like a huge ocean liner. It has many systems where teams of workers perform their daily repetitive tasks that keep the vessel running. The captain is unaware of, and likely has no direct access to, most of them as he performs his own tasks of navigation and keeping external dangers at bay.

Ordinarily there are systems in place to direct the operations of the kitchen crew for example. From his place on the Bridge, the captain has no direct ability to influence their actions; there is no intercom system from the Bridge to the Galley to ask them to make pancakes for tea. However, through focused intent, he can consciously leave the bridge and talk to the kitchen crew directly and have the ships menu altered.

Similarly, there are tools and methods by which one can directly influence every aspect of the human body right down to the smallest detail.

Understanding Your Body

The Brain, the Mind and the Universe

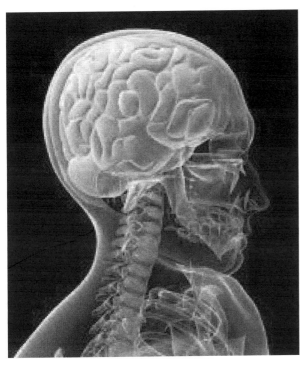

We have been educated, indoctrinated, propagandised to see the world around us in terms of separate physical objects - things - which inherently have physical characteristics such as colour, weight, texture, etc.

This is a world where only the physical exists and consequently we have come to consider ourselves as big strapping physical beings, separate from each other and an environment also made up of separate objects, some squishy and smelly, others brightly coloured and delicious tasting, and still others with large pointy teeth and eyes that look at you in a rather disconcerting way.

In this model of the universe, the brain is regarded as nothing more than a sophisticated computer network, receiving sensory input data from the outside world, organising and analysing the data to determine threats or discover avenues to pleasurable experiences, while simultaneously saving the data to its biological hard drive as memories.

The reality, however, is far stranger. The brain does indeed receive something in the order of four billion bits of information per second, in a stream of electro-chemical signals from our various sensory organs, but this, in itself, poses a very interesting problem.

When we stand in front of a tree, we can see the shape and colour of its trunk and branches, we can smell its fragrance, we can reach out and feel the texture of its bark and hear the rustling of its leaves in the wind, but what is really happening here?

Our eyes are receiving various wavelengths of reflected and emitted light from an object and certain rods and cones on the retinas are stimulated to fire an electro-chemical charge. Some are stimulated more than others, some do not respond at all, but a stream of electrical information is sent to the brain along the optic nerve to represent "sight". Similarly, there are electro-chemical patterns of signals fired off from receptors in our nose, ears and nerve endings embedded in our skin that are "labelled" smell, sound, touch, feel and temperature. And in about a tenth of a second the brain collates all these patterns of electrical information, compares it to other stored pattern templates of "things" that it has been taught about and previously encountered, and retrieves the appropriate labels, and you say:

"Ah, it's a tree."

But here is the point: Have you actually experienced a *"thing"* called a tree? No, your brain has merely created a model of a *"thing"* that it has labelled a tree from a pattern of electrical waveforms. It has internally manufactured qualities such as colour, in order to differentiate between different frequencies of energy in what we call the *"visible light spectrum"*.

Colour does not exist in the *"physical"* world, so the electrical signals flowing along our optic nerves are not green or brown. Colour is an internally generated phenomenon, not an external one, and so is a subjective experience, meaning that your experience of the colour blue is different to everyone else's experience. The confusion arises because we have all agreed to give our subjective experience of *"Blue"* the same label and so erroneously take it to be an objective one. The same holds true for all our other senses, and this provides an easy answer to the age old question:

"If a tree falls in a forest and there is no-one around to hear it, does it make a sound?"

No, it does not make a sound, because we make sound – or rather our brains manufacture a quality that we call sound from a pattern of electrical signals derived from sensitive hairs in our ears that respond to a narrow band of subtle variations of air pressure. When a tree falls, a mass of air molecule vibrations and compressions ensue, but it requires an ear, a nervous system and a brain to convert them into sound.

We have never directly experienced a tree or any other *"thing"* in the *"physical"* world. We interact with an interpretation or conceptual model of the world that our brain creates as a *"best guess"* based on the information it receives and the conceptual pigeonholes provided by our language and culture, and since this model is uniquely personal to you, if I were somehow able to briefly experience your model, it is highly unlikely that I would be able to make any sense of it at all.

We have no idea what lies in the so-called *"physical world"* beyond the boundary of our skin, but it is likely to be a unified, but unimaginable kaleidoscope of energy, in waves of infinite possibilities, not individual, physical *"things"* at all.

As the philosopher Alan Watts once put it:

"A 'thing' is a 'think'"

But, as strange as all that might seem to you, the most incredible is yet to come. Experiments in the fields of Holography, Medical Research and Quantum Physics have revealed a startling picture of our universe.

Quantum Physicists noticed that when they attempted to discover what matter was composed of, they found that it consisted of 99.9999999% empty space and when they examined the particles in that space they found them to be composed of even tinier *"particles"* whizzing around even vaster amounts of empty space, prompting one scientist to remark:

"Whatever matter is made of, it's not matter"

Even more puzzling, is that under certain conditions, the *"particles"* that make up the material world behave like waves of potential with only a probability of appearing in one particular location or another.

Physicists performed the infamous Double Slit Experiment in which they set up an *"Electron Gun"* that can fire single electrons (little bits of matter) through a barrier with a single vertical slit, at a screen.

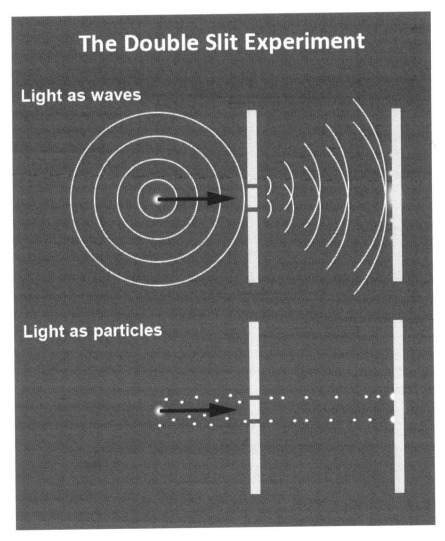

If they then run the experiment and note where the electrons strike the screen, after some time a single line of electron strikes will emerge corresponding with the slit in the barrier, however if they replace the barrier with one containing two slits and repeat the experiment then something strange happens.

Instead of seeing two lines on the screen, a strange pattern of light and dark bands appear, as if the electrons are not behaving like separate bits of matter but more like waves on the ocean. As these waves radiate out from the other side of the slits, where the top of one wave meets the top of another then they reinforce each other and there is a high probability that an electron will strike the screen, but where the top of one wave meets the bottom of another, they cancel each other out and there is a correspondingly low probability that an electron will hit the screen in that position. This pattern is known as an interference pattern - as it is produced when waves interfere with each other.

Physicists were completely baffled, because they were firing separate electrons, one at a time, at the screen. What could they possibly be interfering with?

In an attempt to understand this phenomenon, they placed a detector by one of the slits so that they could tell through which slit an electron will pass, but when they ran the experiment, the screen displayed **two lines** instead of the interference pattern.

The inescapable conclusion is that the electron leaves the electron gun as a wave of possibilities. That is, it can go through either the left slit or the right, or neither, or both at the same time, (which is a possibility, albeit an unlikely one from our *"common sense"* frame of reference) where it interferes with itself to produce and interference pattern. But if a conscious observer has knowledge of which slit the electron actually passes through, then the wave collapses to one definite possibility and behaves as a particle. This conclusion has been borne out time and time again in experiment after experiment, including an intriguing one called the Delayed Quantum Erasure Experiment.

In this experiment, the double slit experiment is performed, but neither the detector data, nor the resulting pattern on the screen are looked at, but rather, are sealed in separate envelopes. These envelopes are sealed in another envelope which is marked *"Experiment One"*, and this is repeated until they have one hundred and two envelopes. The envelopes are then sealed in a safe.

Ten years later, (although the amount of time is unimportant) the first and last experiment envelopes are opened by physicists who were not involved in collecting the data. They looked at the detector data, and they saw two lines on the screen data.

Next, they mixed up the remaining envelopes and chose fifty at random and repeated the exercise, that is, they looked at the detector data, followed by the screen data and each time they see **two lines of particle strikes**. For the remaining fifty experiment envelopes, they destroyed all the unopened detector data envelopes but when they looked at the screen data, in each and every case they found an **interference pattern**.

The interference pattern or undefined wave of possibilities remains because the information that would collapse it to a definite event will no longer exists and so, can never be defined. Just as it requires an eye at a particular location, connected to a conscious mind to evoke a rainbow out of a tangled mass of light frequencies; it requires a mind commanding a battery of sense organs to evoke a *"particular"* reality image out of waves of infinite possibilities, which appears worryingly similar to how a hologram works.

A hologram is created by using a laser of a specific frequency and angle to convert the image of a three dimensional object to an interference wave pattern that is recorded on a holographic plate, such that if another laser of the same frequency is shone on the plate at the same angle, then the interference pattern of waves is collapsed back into the three dimensional image.

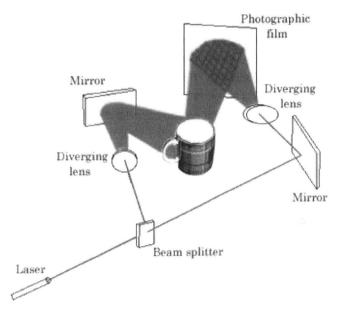

How a Hologram is constructed.

The process by which the pattern of the image is converted into an interference pattern of wave information and back again, can be expressed mathematically by a type of calculus known as Fourier Transforms. It turns out that the brain uses Fourier Transforms to process the electrical patterns of information received from the senses into a holographic three dimensional image which it projects outside of ourselves for us to perceive.

In other words, the brain receives a subset of the infinite possibilities *"out there"* and collapses them down to a hologram of particulate matter, which we perceive outside ourselves as *"real"* because our bodies themselves are also made up of the same holographic particulate matter.

The significance of this in regards to this book is that the condition, appearance, performance and health of your body are a direct reflection of the state of your mind and the belief systems it holds because your body is just a projection of what you believe it to be.

Powerful knowledge, in the hands of those that know how to apply it.

The Thief Who Comes Bearing Gifts

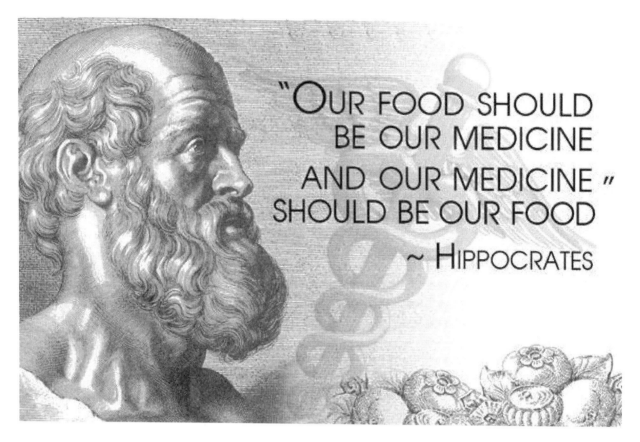

Dude, where's my energy?

The human body operates on a finite amount of energy that it gathers from its environment on a moment to moment basis.

Under ideal conditions, this energy is sufficient to carry out the most strenuous physical tasks as well as perform internal maintenance and repair operations to keep it running at peak efficiency. However, we have been convinced to adopt a pernicious and highly addictive habit which saps up to 80% of the body's energy reserves, under the guise of providing the very energy that it is soaking up. Consequently, since we do not spend the entirety of our day resting, our body is forced to allocate its remaining energy to physical work like walking, lifting, carrying etc., leaving very little for repair and maintenance.

This habit is many times more addictive than crack cocaine and just like all other addictive drugs, it causes unpleasant physiological changes - and often undesirable behavioural changes too; Yet it is so heavily marketed and attractively advertised that most of the human race is completely addicted to it, and if they were to attempt to quit cold turkey from it, they would likely be dead in three to four weeks.

So what is this dangerous narcotic? It is, of course, Food!

I will pause right here because you are probably reading this book with a cup of tea and are now glaring, with suspicion and horror, at the chocolate biscuit, that you were just about to pop in your mouth.

Yes, I said *"Food!"*

But I like Chocolate Biscuits!

The culture within which we live, and the language we use, relentlessly tells us that food provides us with the energy that we require to live and that without it we will starve, emaciate and die a slow, painful and lingering death.

We are bombarded with images of healthy, attractive people enthusiastically gorging themselves on enticingly packaged food-like products, contrasted with horrifying images of children in Africa, starving for the lack of it, but, as Tony Blair once said:

> *"A lie told often enough becomes the truth."*

> (Actually this is a lie, Tony Blair never actually admitted to using this tactic but if I were to repeatedly tell you that he did then you would start to believe me.)

The reality is that, just like the thief who gains entry with gifts of attractive looking trinkets, then quietly proceeds to steal everything of value, the process of digestion expends up to 80% of the body's available energy while providing none.

We are intuitively aware of the truth, but our (programmed) logical minds suppress it. Ask yourself how you feel after having over-eaten a large Christmas meal? Do you feel energised, lively and bursting with energy, or do you feel tired, sleepy, lethargic and lazy?

As we will see later, digestion is a highly energy intensive process of emergency elimination and when we subject ourselves to three square meals a day we unwittingly reduce our energy levels to 20% for the entire day, that is barely enough to keep our bodies functioning.

When an internal problem arises, our body begins to deal with it and it alerts us to the issue with physical manifestations that the medical establishment terms *"symptoms,"* and we are said to have become ill. Our intuitive response is to stop eating and rest, but once again our culture, language and programming kicks in with the idea:

> *"You have to eat to keep your strength up."*

Our mothers feed us Chicken soup, robbing us of the energy we were using to deal with the illness; we ingest a pharmaceutical symptom suppressant so that we are no longer aware that there is a problem; and we go on about our day, expending the little energy we have left while, behind the scenes, the problem that caused the "illness" in the first place, builds and compounds until it manifests in some other, more catastrophic way.

It becomes obvious why it seems as though we struggle to recover from illness and disease, we simply do not have the energy.

*   *   *   *

There is a very good reason why we like our chocolate biscuits, pizzas and thousands of other delicacies and tasty treats: On top of their inherently addictive qualities and enhanced by slick advertising, the food corporations employ legions of chemical engineers to fool the body into wanting more. A good example of this occurred in 2012, when it was revealed that scientists working for Pepsi were using human tissue from aborted foetal cells to develop flavour enhancing chemicals for their products.

Increasingly, through the use of the mass media and psychological techniques, we are also being steered away from natural foods towards processed food analogues, which are literally no more than chemical compounds and textural extracts designed to trick the addict's mind into believing it is food - and yet leave him feeling empty with the desire to eat more.

The chemicals employed in these *"food similar"* products induce symptoms in the human body in order to generate profits for the symptom suppressant arm of their cartel of corporations.

Don't take it personally, it's just business!

When Hippocrates said,

"Let food be thy medicine and medicine be thy food"

I believe he was speaking literally. It may be the case that the first foods we ingested were medicines. Indeed, when certain herbs and plants come into contact with the skin or are ingested, they stimulate specific internal reactions within the body which can suppress the symptoms of the body's normal healing processes. Some of these medicines were so pleasurable to the taste that a habit formed – just like some people today, get addicted to the taste of cough medicine.

In his book, *"Man's Higher Consciousness"*, Professor Hilton Hotema described the decline of man from a "perfect" state of **Breatharian**, which is one who requires no food or water; down in stages to the sickly, short-lived imperfect beings we are now.

Breatharian • Liquidarian • Fruitarian • Vegetarian • Carnivore

Hotema maintained that our lifespans originally measured thousands of years but as we descended these stages, taking on denser and denser material matter, our bodies had to adjust to these new destructive habits at the expense of our longevity. These habits have subsequently been manipulated and stimulated using Pavlovian psychological techniques, by those who profit from supplying the addicts they create and control.

As Henry Kissinger, one of the architects (or pawns) of the global Orwellian nightmare we inhabit, puts it,

"Food is a weapon."

What's Your Poison?

The simple fact is that all food is poisonous. We know intuitively that some of the things which we put in our mouths are toxic to the body, such as caffeine, sugar, salt and alcohol, but even some of the food items that we consider as harmless or even *"nutritious"* are in fact toxic to some extent and even though they may not kill you immediately, they do so slowly, by degrees.

The common potato, for example, is descended from the deadly nightshade family, if the poisonous alkaloids it contains are not cooked out to a tolerable level, it can cause *"potato poisoning"*. The tomato also belongs to the same family and the vines of both plants are so deadly that few animals will eat them.

Garlic and onion contain a sedative substance and oil which irritates the eyes, kidneys, bladder and the genital mucous membrane.

Lettuce also contains a sedative and a harmful alkaloid called *"lactucarium"*, a powerful narcotic that is sometimes used as a substitute for opium.

Asparagus, celery, cabbage, onions and turnips all contain saltpeter, an ingredient in gunpowder.

Cabbage and turnips both contain arsenic, while beets, eggplant, spinach, swiss chard and rhubarb contain other poisons.

Even the tools of the herbalist are harmful to the body. The application or ingestion of certain plants stimulate marked reactions in the body, irritating it by virtue of their toxicity, but it was undoubtedly noticed that some of these reactions appeared to be beneficial in suppressing symptoms and so these particular plants are labelled as *"medicinal herbs"*. While some herbal remedies can be useful, we will see later why suppressing symptoms or introducing any form of toxicity to the body are not necessarily conducive to healing.

Other plants have such a powerful smell or taste that we label them as *"culinary herbs"* or *"spices"* and we use them to add flavour to other foods, but these strong odours are usually an indication of the level of toxicity developed as a strategy by the plants to deter insects from eating them.

Culinary herbs and spices are used to make ordinarily unpalatable foods edible, salt was originally a preservative for meat to stop it rotting, and most other spices and condiments found their way on to our dinner tables in an attempt to disguise the taste of rotting food with even stronger flavours.

If that were not enough, the pesticides that are used in non-organically grown produce are not only harmful to insects but equally harmful to humans too.

Pesticides originated as chemical and biological weapons that could kill thousands of people in great clouds of poison gas. When world war two ended and there were no more human enemies to kill, the large chemical corporations that had made huge profits from the slaughter were left with large stockpiles of chemical weapons. So in order to keep the profits rolling in, these weapons were repackaged and sold as pesticides for the very plausible reason that they kill insects that feed on the crops, but the truth is that they continue to serve their original purpose of killing humans, but this time in their millions, slowly and quietly.

At this point most people will ask:

> *"What **can** I eat that isn't going to do harm to my body then?"*

The simple answer is *"Nothing!"*

Everything that you put into your mouth will require your body to react in one way or another, to compensate for the damage it causes, at the cost of its vitality and longevity.

But since we are all addicted to eating, the very best that most of us can do is to steer our diets toward the uppermost portion of Hotema's stages of decline.

If we were to confine our consumption habit to water and raw organically grown fruit (which is mainly water anyway) then we limit the damage caused by it and reduce the amount of energy required to eliminate it from our system.

The chocolate biscuit, which I hope you haven't eaten yet, is likely to contain:

- **Wood Pulp**: to provide most of its bulk and texture.
- **Wheat Glutens**: which can cause bloating, constipation, diarrhoea, weight loss, fat malabsorption and malnutrition (iron deficiency or anaemia), osteoporosis, intestinal permeability (leaky gut), systemic inflammation and autoimmune disease (celiac disease).
- **Partially Hydrogenated Oils**: contain Trans fatty acids, which raise bad cholesterol and lower good cholesterol, and contribute to heart disease.
- **Soya Lecithin**: Soy bean oil waste sludge which causes digestive distress, immune system breakdown, PMS, endometriosis, and reproductive problems for men and women; ADD and ADHD; higher risk of heart disease and cancer; malnutrition and loss of libido; and also triggers severe allergic reactions.
- **High Fructose Corn Syrup**: accelerates the aging process; triggers asthma, food allergies, multiple sclerosis and other immune system problems; causes Metabolic syndrome and Mercury poisoning; and increases risk for type 2 diabetes, coronary heart disease, stroke and cancer.
- **Aspartame**: formally a biological warfare chemical developed by the Pentagon, it is quite literally a bacteriological excrement that destroys brain cells, but stimulates certain taste-buds to register the quality of intense sweetness.
- **Natural Vanilla Flavouring**: a substance called "castoreum" that is, believe it or not, a secretion from the **anal gland of a Beaver**, with which they mark their territory.

Please, put down and step away from the chocolate biscuit.

The Myth of Nutrition

The very idea that Man is not meant to eat has far reaching implications and also raises many questions, but I will attempt to show that it is the idea of nutrition is a myth - One propagated by an incorrect (if not fraudulent) interpretation of observed phenomena.

The first myth to dispel is that the food we eat goes inside our bodies, provides nutrition and builds up our body by becoming part of it. First of all, food does not actually enter **into** our body.

Now, I know what you are thinking;

> *"Of course it goes inside us, I eat an apple and in ends up inside my body... duh!"*

I understand how that would appear to be the case, but consider, if you will, a doughnut.

Mmmmm, doughnuts....

The outside of the doughnut is a nice crispy golden brown colour, and the inside is a gooey, creamy off white colour. Everywhere you look on the doughnut you are looking at the outside of it, even when you look down the hole in the centre.

Now imagine the doughnut stretched out into a long tube shape, even now, when you look down into the hole, you are still looking at the outside of the doughnut. Put a set of teeth on the top end and a hole on the bottom, and topologically, you have the human body. Food does not go inside us, it goes through us. Our intestinal tract is made up of modified skin cells and our stomach is merely a bulge in the tube.

Food does not provide nutrition; it merely acts as an agent to stimulate a reaction in the body.

Imagine you were walking through a forest and your arm accidentally comes into contact with some stinging nettles.

A chemical reaction takes place on the skin's surface; however, inside the body, several processes are stimulated into action - such as: increased blood flow to the area; a histamine response; an increase in white blood cells; nerve endings firing to register irritation; all resulting in a painful welt under the skin. The nettles did not enter the body nor become part of it; they did nothing more than cause an external chemical reaction which provoked an internal response.

Eating from the Senna plant, for example, irritates the bowels to cause them to quickly release their contents, often in amusingly embarrassing ways. The medical priesthood labels Senna as a laxative, falsely attributing its action to an inherent effect of the plant - rather than to a reaction in the body, to the irritation caused by the plant. It's a subtle distinction, but one that follows the common practice of placing the power externally in expensive pharmaceuticals, pills and potions, rather than as a natural function of the human body.

When we eat, 99% of the food, having produced its chemical reactions during the chemical interplay of digestion, passes out of the body. A small amount of the chemical components of the food do - indeed get absorbed into the body, but these too, perform a stimulant action upon the organs before they pass out of the body. In fact, if you were to carefully weigh everything that you consume, you would find that it would almost exactly match what you would pass out.

People do indeed die from, what is termed starvation, but that is not due to a lack of nutrition, but rather, a lack of stimulation to a body that has become so accustomed to stimulus, that it can no longer perform many of its vital functions without particular types of stimuli to initiate them.

The use of heroin stimulates the release of endorphins and other *"feel good"* hormones. However, as it is used more and more, the body becomes less able to manufacture the endorphins by itself and begins to depend on the heroin stimulation to initiate the endorphin release. Before long, the addict can no longer feel good - or indeed function properly - without it.

So the addict is forced to take more and more heroin, in ever increasing amounts in order just to function, and eventually the addict will get to the stage where, if he were to stop taking the drug, he would die from a lack of something that the body ordinarily has absolutely no use for.

* * * *

Just in case this section left you with a desire for doughnuts, here is a picture of a beaver's bottom:

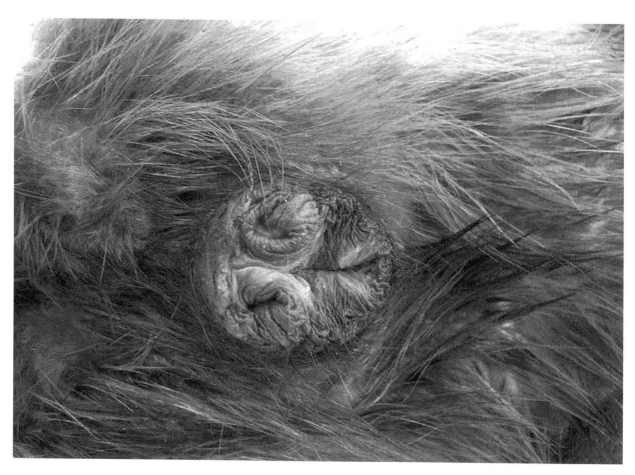

Mmmmm, vanilla...

Make like a tree and leave

"So if all our food passes straight through us, how do we grow?"

I'm glad you asked me that.

The human body is made up of trillions of cells, but none of them were built from food. Each and every one of them came from the one original parent cell that divided and subdivided and so on and so forth. Cells do not eat. Each one is a self-sustaining being, and a microcosm of the larger being which it helps comprise. The cell is made up of molecules that also do not require food, which in turn are comprised of atoms and electrons, neither of which consume a thing.

In the same way that invisible water vapour can condense into solid ice, the human body condenses all its material needs from the field of electro-magnetic radiation that surrounds us, at the particular frequency required for any given substance.

The very same process happens all around us in nature. Trees do not get nourishment from the soil, otherwise you would see every large tree growing out of a depression in the earth, that would be formed as it took nutrients from the soil beneath it; and in fact, trees and plants contain elements that are not found in the soil around them.

A plant grown inside a sealed glass bottle, thriving despite not having water or fresh air for 40 years.

In the 17th century, Jean Van Helmont performed an experiment to test this. He placed two hundred pounds of soil in a ceramic pot, and then planted a Willow tree weighing five pounds into it. After five years of only adding distilled water or rainwater, the tree had grown to be over six feet high, and weighed one hundred and sixty nine pounds, but yet the weight of the soil in the pot remained completely unchanged.

"So where did all that wood come from?"

It came from the elements condensed from cosmic radiation. The process by which plants and trees convert light into plant matter is labelled by the scientific deities as *"photosynthesis"*.

Russian engineer and scientist Georges Lakhovsky also demonstrated that food supplies no energy and is not responsible for organic growth or maintenance.

31

In one experiment, Lakhovsky measured the amount of iron contained in a colony of single cell organisms and sealed them in a test tube. After a period of growth he found that the amount of iron had increased as the cells multiplied, despite being in a completely sealed environment. This proves that it is the body's own physiological processes that convert cosmic radiation into proteins, minerals and other substances - not food.

The human body uses its own version of photosynthesis to convert cosmic radiation (light) into human matter.

This explanation also answers the same inevitable question that is often posed by the poor meat eater that has been cornered by a ravenous pack of vegans who have caught the scent of lettuce and tomatoes on their victim:

"What about protein? Where would the body get its protein from?"

Once again, it is common indoctrination that has superseded common sense.

If it were not the case that the body manufactures all the protein that it requires, then how is it that a protein packed beef steak comes from an animal that eats mainly grass? How can it be that the largest, most powerful animals in the African jungle, the Elephant, Rhinoceros and Gorilla, are all vegetarians?

I would cordially invite any three muscle-bound, meat eating bodybuilders, who still maintain that protein is absolutely necessary to build muscle, into a ring against your average fully grown Gorilla.

My money would be on the vegetarian.

I'm pink, therefore I'm ham

You can see that our *"common sense"* view is based on an incorrect interpretation of observed phenomena, due to flawed logic and selective emphasis on some evidence - while ignoring that which does not conform. We see food going into the body, and we see that body growing and doing work, and so we make the erroneous - yet seemingly logical - cause and effect correlation between the two.

Along those same lines, another obvious question often asked at this point is:

> *"If we weren't meant to eat, why do we have a digestive system?"*

This question falls into a similar logical trap because it implies that we eat because we have a digestive system. That statement disregards the fact that the human body is designed to be extremely adaptable, and ignores the possibility that we just might have a digestive system **because** we started eating.

The human body contains many organs that do not appear to serve any useful function, such as the tonsils and the appendix. The medical mobsters will tell you that perhaps at one time they served a purpose but now they are merely redundant organs, which they will not hesitate to whip out at the first sign of trouble. But their logic does not take into account the fact that the human body is intelligent and adaptable, and it is that very **adaptability** which is the purpose they serve.

If, for instance, you were to start eating grass as a habit, the first thing that would happen is you would become violently sick as the body is not equipped to handle it. However, if you were to persist in this habit then your dynamic and intelligent body would begin to adapt to accommodate you. It would suppress the urge to vomit (which serves as a warning indicator) and over time, your appendix would enlarge and begin processing the grass. If your habits were to change again and you stopped eating grass, then your appendix would shrink and become a redundant organ once more.

Interestingly, the first thing that happens when one stops eating for any length of time, is that the stomach and digestive tract start to shrink; it would follow that if one gave up eating altogether, then they too would become redundant organs about which some future allopathic doctor might say,

> *"You have a stomach ulcer; I'm going to recommend you have surgery to remove the stomach and digestive system. They are redundant organs., Actually we're not quite sure what they are for, but you don't need them."*

Another question that is based on circumstantial evidence, taken as proof is:

> *"Why then, does my stomach rumble when I get hungry and I don't eat?"*

This viewpoint presupposes that we accept the Newtonian view that the human body is just a blind mechanism, like a clockwork toy, rather than a dynamic, intelligent system.

The answer is simple and rather obvious. If you were to eat lunch every day at 12:30 p.m. then your body will respond to this pattern of behaviour such that by 12:20 p.m. the amount of saliva and gastric juices secreted would be elevated in anticipation. The noises emanating from your stomach would be a result of the increased levels of stomach acids with nothing to digest, rather than an indication of hunger.

Hunger is somewhat of an illusion, and as anyone who has fasted for a week or more knows, appetite comes with eating. That's not to say that people do not starve to death. As alluded to earlier, sudden changes to the body are dangerous - but given enough time to adapt to the situation, one can be weaned off food altogether.

Something in the Air

The human body's energy does not come from the combustion of food. If it did, then we would have no options for extra bursts of energy in an emergency situation, while on an empty stomach. So it would seem logical that a way to determine the source of the energy would be to examine what happens when a human has to expend a significant amount of it.

At rest, the average adult inhales about 500 cubic inches of air per minute; this figure rises to around 2500 cubic inches of air per minute if he walks four miles an hour; it increases to about 3500 cubic inches if he walks six miles an hour: and after a long run he would find himself breathing rather heavily.

It is quite apparent that our oxygen intake keeps pace with our energy requirements in a direct correlation. There is no such relationship between food intake and energy expenditure.

A human could fast for 40 days with no loss of energy (in fact he would find a significant energy boost for reasons previously explained) and would still retain the capacity for emergency bursts of energy to, say, escape from a predator. However, if the breathing were to be interrupted for any more than a few minutes, the body will lose all energy, then lose consciousness, and very quickly lose its connection to life.

Free Energy

The body likewise generates a significant amount of electrical energy that also does not appear to originate from the chemical energy in food, or any obvious molecular interaction from its oxygen intake. To find the source of this energy, one must look further afield to the world of Free Energy.

In the 1890's, Nicola Tesla had just invented alternating current, and while the whole world was focused on his new power transmission medium, he turned his attention back to studying direct current, and in particular, why it was that operators of large DC motors would often be electrocuted by a bright blue white electrical discharge when they threw the switch.

After some study Tesla found that he could recreate this effect by pulsing high voltage direct current at very high speeds, but what he discovered was actually a different form of energy - which he called "Radiant Energy."

Radiant Energy, resembled a bright blue white spark of electricity, but behaved more like a gas that flowed on the surface of the wires that carried it, and also exhibited many other strange and wonderful properties.

As Tesla increased the frequency of the pulses generated by his radiant energy device, he found that the room would light up as the air molecules themselves would begin to luminesce. When he pushed the pulse rate higher, the air would give off infra-red radiation, causing the room to warm up and at even higher frequencies cooling breezes would move around the room.

Over 100 years later, an inventor named John Bedini released a Free Energy device which charged batteries by channelling spikes of this Radiant Energy into them.

In the documentary series "Energy From The Vacuum", Bedini explains that his device does not charge batteries in the conventional way. Rather, it generates spikes of radiant energy and when those spikes hit the electro-chemical makeup of the battery, the battery is able to draw in energy from the vacuum (the ether, or the zero point field) which manifests as an electrical charge.

He goes on to note that the radiant energy spikes that his device produces are **identical** to nerve impulses in the human body.

The implication is clear - we do not run on chemical energy derived from food at all. We run on vacuum energy, and our nerve impulses interact with our own electro-chemical makeup, and we draw in the energy we need from the space around us.

* * * *

The perfect human body, one untainted by the unhealthy habits of "civilisation", is a self sufficient unit that does not require any external input for its survival, just like the cells that make up the body and the atoms that comprise the cell do not need food to power them. The Earth, of which the human body itself is just a cell, likewise does not eat food, neither does the solar system, the galaxy or the universe as a whole.

Given a favourable environment, the human body manufactures all of its material needs in the correct amounts to ensure the body's equilibrium and optimum health. All so-called deficiencies and imbalances are the result of adjustments to an inhospitable environment and the action of ingested foodstuffs that stimulate the over-production of some necessary substances and suppress the production of others.

If one were to eat foods that stimulate the stomach to overproduce digestive acids, the body would compensate by extracting Calcium (which is the most efficient antacid available to it) from the bones and other sources, and voila, you have a (temporary) calcium deficiency. Not because of a lack of milk or calcium supplements, but from a seemingly unrelated event that caused the body to redistribute its resources in an emergency situation.

Ingesting inorganic forms of these minerals in the form of supplements is like chewing nails to correct an iron deficiency.

Supplements do not correct deficiencies, if the body is left unhindered, the deficiency will correct itself, however, the inorganic minerals contained within the supplements will eventually accumulate in various parts of the body and cause further problems

In short, food, is not our friend!

The Waste Management System

There have been many experiments that show that the elimination of toxic substances from the body is far more important than this idea of nutrition. Records have shown that people have lived without food from anywhere between forty days and forty years, but if you were to suppress the body's ability to eliminate toxic substances, the body could not last more than a few minutes.

Let's take a look at why elimination much more vitally important than nutrition.

The Immortal Body

The cells of the human body renew themselves by dividing and discarding part of themselves like a snake shedding its skin. They also change in response to changes in their environment.

In ideal conditions, the cell will perfectly receive the eternal, animating stream of consciousness that is you. However, should the environment become polluted the ability of that cell to receive your consciousness degrades until it reaches a level below which it can no longer receive the signal of the animating spirit and so becomes inanimate. At this point we say that the cell has died. Their magnetic poles become corroded by the acidic substances that are not carried off and eliminated by a clogged blood stream.

The human body is composed of cells, and given the proper environment the cells of the body are, for all intents and purposes, immortal. They do not die.

The great physiologist and Nobel Prize winner, Dr. Alexis Carrel, stated in his work *"Man, The Unknown"*:

"The cell is immortal. It is merely the fluid in which it floats that degenerates. Renew this fluid at proper intervals, and give the cell proper nourishment upon which to feed, and, so far as we know, the pulsation of life may go on forever."

Carrel's Wikipedia entry, with regards to his work on Cellular senescence, notes his experiment that ran between 1912 and 1940 where he kept cells from a chicken heart alive for 28 years just by keeping its environment optimal, even though a chicken only lives on average 8 years. He concluded that cells are immortal, and it's just the fluid that it floats in degenerates. Renew this fluid and life will continue indefinitely. The Wikipedia article then goes on to dismiss this evidence and echo the medical establishments view of the *"aging"* of cells by stating:

*"He (Carrel) claimed **incorrectly** that all cells continue to grow indefinitely"*

This article claims that Carrel's experiment was never successfully replicated and so his results were labelled as anomalous and his conclusions replaced by an unproven theory that cells can only undergo a finite number of divisions before they die. Despite all evidence to the contrary the medical and scientific mafia has adopted this as the foundation of biology.

The Cells from HELA

Henrietta Lacks

In 1951, a 31 year old black woman from Baltimore, named Henrietta Lacks, died of a highly malignant strain of cervical cancer.

Pieces of her tumour were used in tissue cell culture. At that time previous attempts to grow human cells had been unsuccessful, however, this time they kept the cells in a concoction of human placenta blood, an extract of cattle embryo and fresh chicken blood plasma and the cells continued to grow. They did not age or die instead they found that if they *"fed"* the cells properly, or rather provide the correct environment for the cells then they could live and multiply indefinitely just as Carrel predicted.

The scientific and medical priesthood are very careful not to present this phenomenon in terms of cell immortality; instead they describe how these cells are:

"...unusually resilient, for reasons scientists still don't fully understand"

Implying that out of all the cells in the living universe, these particular cancer cells from a dead black woman are so virulent that they alone cannot age and die.

This is plainly ridiculous. There are no *"special cases"* in nature. It is obvious that Carrel's view that as long as the environment within which the cell floats is healthy the cell will continue indefinitely is the more accurate picture.

Despite their impossibility, these immortal cancer cells, known as HELA cells from the name of their original donor **HE**nrietta **LA**cks, are well known amongst the scientific and medical cartels. Apparently, over 60 years after her death, Lacks' tissue has yielded around 50 million metric tons of HELA cells and scientific and medical researchers publish about 300 HELA related studies each month contributing to a library of 60,000 such studies.

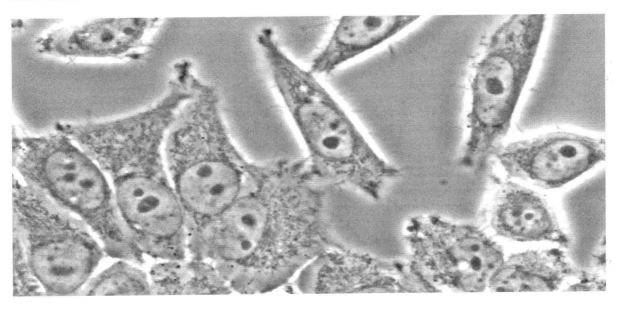

HELA Cells

Why would the medical establishment around the world require so much of these highly dangerous cancer cells?

Well, the white coats claim that it has been invaluable in studying and facilitating the process of viral recombination, horizontal gene transfer and other esoteric subjects that causes reader's eyes to glaze over and make them feel like nipping off to make a cup of tea. However, one might, if so inclined, want to ask why, strangely enough, almost all promising cancer research cultures have been found to be contaminated with this very particular strain of cells, according to Walter Nelson-Rees, a cell culture expert. Or why every vaccine produced anywhere in the world also appear to be contaminated with the highly malignant cancer cells of a black woman from Baltimore who died because of them.

But I digress; the important thing to remember here is that as long as the cell's environment is healthy then the cells will live on indefinitely.

The River of Life

The environment within which the cells float is of course, the blood, and we find, in the study of the blood, that Carrel's assertion is echoed by other leading scientists of his day.

The famous nineteenth century Russian scientist Ilya Metchnikoff presented, in his book, "*Prolongation of Life*" a well reasoned explanation of the degenerative changes he saw in the human body. He directly attributed the phenomena of old age and the deterioration of the bodily structure to minute quantities of poisonous substances in the blood.

Similarly, in Bernarr Macfadden's 1910 book, "*Vitality Supreme*", he wrote:

> *"If we maintain our blood in normal condition and circulation, sickness would be almost impossible. The blood is the life of the flesh. We are what we are by the influence of our blood flowing thru our body"*

The blood is a transportation system, the essence of everything that one breathes, drinks and eats enter the body and pass into the blood. The blood carries oxygen to the cells to power them and carries off carbon dioxide, the poisonous exhaust from this process. The substances absorbed from food stimulate and activate the cells by virtue of being poisonous or a chemical irritant.

There is also another critical function that the blood performs and that is to carry off the toxic products of cell disintegration.

Every day, millions of cells *"die"* and are renewed through the process of cell division. As the discarded parts of these cells decompose, they produce a number of toxic substances including carbonic, lactic, hydrochloric and phosphoric acids. The blood must also remove these acidic poisons .

So while the blood is a life giving river of health and vitality it is at the same time a stagnant pool of poison and death, which it must dispose of quickly and efficiently in case it poisons and causes the cells to degenerate.

The venal blood is so loaded with acids and other toxins that it is almost black in colour but as it enters the air sacs of the lungs, in a flash the poisons are exchanged for oxygen and the blood is instantly transformed to a bright scarlet colour. So let's look at some of the systems in place to remove the toxic substances that poison the cell's environment.

The Lungs

Although it seems that the only purpose of the lungs is to supply oxygen to the blood, the other vitally important function that is largely ignored is the expulsion of carbon dioxide and the elimination of toxic products of cell disintegration. Every exhalation is the leading form of excretion. If the lungs were to suddenly stop purifying the blood for just a few minutes, then the result would be death. According to Hilton Hotema, the amount of carbon dioxide that the lungs eliminate over the course of a day would equal an eight ounce lump of charcoal.

When we are in a closed environment with inadequate ventilation, such as our homes when they are virtually sealed shut to keep out winter's chill, we find ourselves breathing the same air over and over and we slowly poison ourselves with the products of our own bodily functions.

French Physiologist, Claude Bernard, once hailed as *"one of the greatest of all men of science"*, performed an experiment where he placed a sparrow in a two litre bell jar which contained enough air to allow it to breathe the products of its own respiration for three hours. After two hours the sparrow was still lively but when it was removed and a second sparrow was introduced to this two hour old air, it died almost immediately in an environment that the original bird, which had grown accustomed to the deteriorating atmosphere, could survive for another hour.

Interestingly though, if the atmosphere were to be maintained at the two hour level of toxicity, then the sparrow that had become accustomed to it, would continue to survive as its body would have adapted itself to tolerate the poisonous air. However, this adaptation to a hostile environment comes at a price: the sparrow's vitality and lifespan would have decreased accordingly.

The human body is larger and far more sophisticated than that of a sparrow and has methods to deal with, and alert you to, mild forms of this auto-intoxication, and we call them coughing and sneezing. These are two natural, emergency processes of violent elimination to expel poisonous gases and acids from the lungs by convulsive motions that propel these gases forcefully out of the lungs. Unfortunately, as previously noted, we, in our ignorance, take pharmaceutical poisons which suppress these functions, halting the elimination of the poisons already in our blood and allow us to comfortably continue to breathe the progressively toxic air and increase the levels of blood toxicity.

As the toxicity increases the body employs other, more drastic processes to eliminate the poisons. We experience them as drowsiness, feelings of restlessness, oppression and unease, headaches, sore throat and fevers. If these indications are ignored or suppressed, the body adopts even more desperate measures to eliminate the now lethal levels of intoxication, the medical highwaymen have called these measures colds, influenza, pneumonia, whooping cough, diphtheria, mumps, measles, scarlet fever.

These are not *"diseases"* caused by some external virus or bacteria, but a chronic state of auto-intoxication resulting in an emergency cleansing response, and the only reason that these conditions appear to be contagious is that those close to the sufferer are also breathing the same toxic air.

We have become accustomed to breathing the toxic air of so-called *"civilisation"* with its pollution, petrochemical fumes, chemical out gassing and stratospheric chemical spraying, and like sparrows in Claude Bernard's bell jar, our general health, vitality and longevity has suffered as a result.

One of the reasons why exercise is such a healthy activity is because it promotes deep, heavy breathing, increasing the elimination of toxins in the blood. However, it is counterproductive if the air that we inhale is just as poisonous as the air that we exhale.

The Liver

All of the blood leaving the stomach and intestinal tract passes through the liver. The liver processes this blood, breaking down the chemicals, toxins and drugs in the blood.

The liver is the primary biochemical synthesiser and detoxifying organ. Its main responsibility is for removing toxins and waste from your blood, processing various chemical stimulants to produce hundreds of bio chemicals, and to activate and regulate important hormones and enzymes that your body needs for daily functioning.

The liver regulates most chemical levels in the blood and, when the liver has broken down poisonous substances, they are excreted as a substance called bile which helps carry away waste and break down fats in the small intestine during digestion and ultimately leave the body in the faeces.

Many vital functions have been identified with the liver. Some of the more well-known functions include the production of blood plasma proteins, Cholesterol, Iron, important vitamins and immune factors, the removal of bacteria from the bloodstream, the regulation of amino acids in the blood, and the conversion of poisonous ammonia to urea, the excess of which is excreted in the urine.

If the liver were to stop purifying the blood then death would follow within three to five days.

The Skin

The skin is a permeable covering of the body that is connected with a vast network of nerves, arteries and veins, and it contains billions of tiny openings called pores. The skin is also the largest organ of elimination of poisonous substances from cell function.

There is an urban legend that actress Shirley Eaton died from skin asphyxiation after having her skin painted with gold paint for the film *"Goldfinger"*.

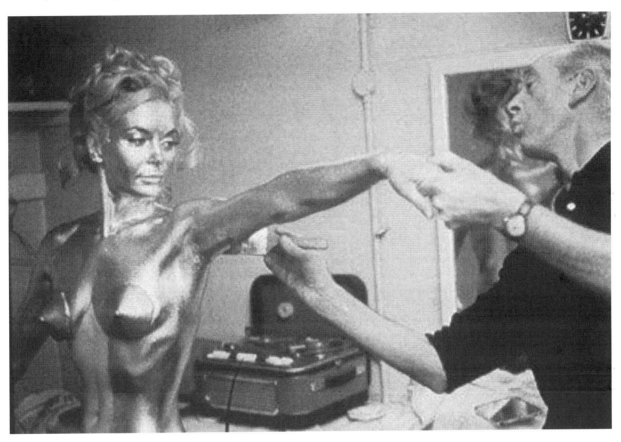

Actress, Shirley Eaton being "primed" for her role in Goldfinger

She did not die, because people do not breathe through the skin, this was a concept made up by Ian Fleming. However, the actress was at grave risk of death because the skin is an organ of elimination of poisonous substances and she risked automatic poisoning of the body because the toxic gases created by cell degradation would not be able to be eliminated through the skin as the pores would be blocked by the paint.

Fortunately for Ms. Eaton, the producers were sufficiently worried by Fleming's skin breathing concept that they left a large square of her skin unpainted which probably saved her life. A similar event was recorded during a papal inauguration in Rome: a small child was painted all over with gold paint so as to look like a cherub and died within twenty minutes from auto poisoning.

These cases show how poisonous carbon dioxide is to the body if it is not eliminated through the lungs and skin. It also shows that the lungs are greatly aided by the skin in the elimination of this deadly gas.

The Kidneys

The kidneys are an exception but are included here for completeness as they do not perform an eliminatory role, rather they act upon already purified blood to remove the excess of the beneficial substances in the blood as urine.

General Practitioners, and even some more senior doctors, will nonetheless parrot the official "wisdom" that urine is a dangerous waste product. However, those who have actually studied the topic will readily admit that the expulsion of urine is a regulatory process and not an elimination of toxins.

This is a quote from Dr. Cameron, Professor of Renal Medicine, Guy's Hospital London:

> *"The principal function of the kidney is not excretion but regulation... The kidney obviously conserves what we need, but even more permits us the freedom of excess. That is, it allows us to take in more than we need of many necessities - water and salt for example - and excretes exactly what is not required"*
>
> "Your Own Perfect Medicine" by Martha Christie (p24)

The kidneys perform a vital function, as too much of any substance in the blood is just as bad as not having enough. If one were to drink a good deal of water then too much would be absorbed into the bloodstream and threaten its optimum performance if not for the kidneys siphoning off the excess into the bladder.

*   *   *   *

We have seen how the eliminatory pathways clear the blood of toxic products and how the kidneys work to keep the blood in perfect balance. The blood is the environment within which the cells of the body float. As long as it remains pure and healthy, the cells will be healthy and, by extension, so will the body.

Trust Me, I'm a Doctor

There is a myth perpetrated by the scientific and medical establishments, aided in no small part by the media, that the science of medicine has been steadily improving the health and life spans of humanity, curing diseases and generally improving the quality of our lives.

Unfortunately the track record of medical science has been less than stellar.

Between the years 1332 and 1382, before there was organised medicine, the Bubonic Plague claimed a total of seventy five million lives in Europe, at a rate of fifteen million people a year.

Five hundred and thirty six years later in 1919, nearly ten years after the establishment of the current allopathic medical system, Spanish Flu killed twenty one million people in less than a year, and by 2030, after one hundred and twenty years of medical advances and the supposed pinnacle of the medical art, fifty six million people worldwide are expected to die of Cancer. So, there is no evidence that the medical establishment has done anything to save lives since its inception. Even Polio, their prized example of the efficacy of vaccines, was actually in decline long before the vaccine was introduced.

The graphs, shown below, depict the official number of deaths as registered in the Official Year Books of Australia, and are taken from Greg Beattie's book *"Vaccination: A Parent's Dilemma"* and clearly show how death rates from infectious disease in Australia were in decline long before vaccines appeared, and the same decline in death rates from infectious disease is evident in America, England, New Zealand and many other countries.

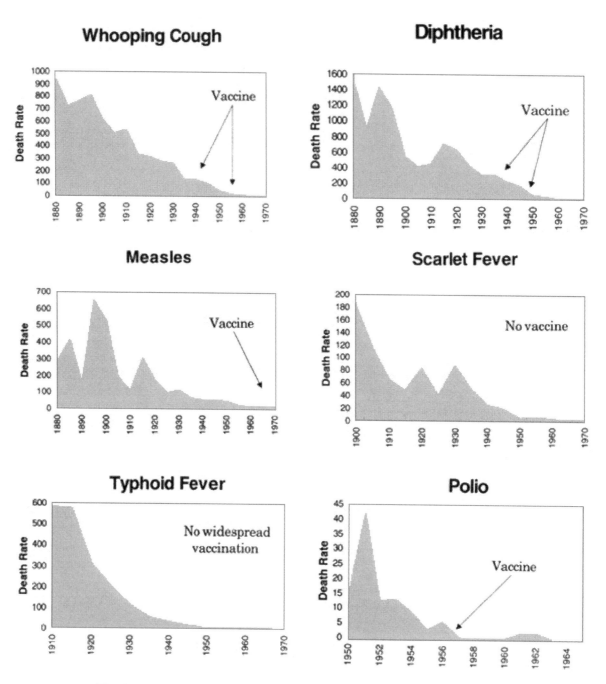

The fraudulent claim that vaccines have an effect on disease outbreaks.

Dr Andrew Weil, in his book, "*Health and Healing*" gives the best explanation of this decline when he said;

> "*Scientific medicine has taken credit it does not deserve for some advances in health. Most people believe that victory over the infectious diseases of the last century came with the invention of immunisations. In fact, cholera, typhoid, tetanus, diphtheria and whooping cough, etc, were in decline before vaccines for them became available - the result of better methods of sanitation, sewage disposal, and distribution of food and water.*"

Despite the overwhelming evidence to the contrary, doctors will wax lyrical about the efficacy of vaccinations, hailing them as one of the great strides of modern medicine and will invariably urge you to have yourself injected as a safeguard against almost anything from the measles/mumps/rubella (MMR), swine flu, cervical cancer to ebola or literally, anything with which they can frighten you into taking it.

Sometimes, doctors can be very, very insistent that you or perhaps your child accept their vaccinations, some may use scare tactics, others will claim that it is mandatory or required by law, nonetheless they have a whole arsenal of techniques to coerce you into compliance. Fortunately there are many strategies to deal with this situation which place the responsibility or burden of proof with the doctor, where it belongs.

If you like to watch a doctor squirm, then you might like to say something like this:

> *"If you are certain that the vaccine is completely safe, then you won't mind taking it first, in front of me, then I will happily take it after you."*

However, if you prefer a less confrontational approach that clearly states your concerns, and allows the doctor ample opportunity to provide proof of his claims and to take responsibility for his actions (which is what he should be doing in any case, right?)

1. Prepare a version of the following *"Notice of Conditional Acceptance"* and *"Liability Statement"* and send to your doctor, recorded delivery.
2. When he does not reply with proofs of claim and a signed liability statement after seven days, then send a reminder (also recorded delivery) giving him a further seven days to respond.
3. After the seven day period expires send a final notice entitled "Notice of Estoppel", explaining all that has transpired, and how that you are now agreed that no proof of claim exists and that it is the doctor's medical opinion that the proposed vaccination is not safe.

The beauty of this approach is that in order to maintain the veneer of full disclosure and plausible deniability should any further action ensue, the doctor will have to prove his position or explain why he failed to do so when given a reasonable opportunity.

Notice of Conditional Acceptance

Dear Dr. **[Doctor's Name]**,

Thank you for insisting that I receive the **[Vaccine Name]** vaccine, you concern for my welfare is most touching.

I am happy to receive this and any such vaccines that you care to administer, on the condition that you provide the following:

1. At least, one double-blind, placebo-controlled study that proves the safety and effectiveness of vaccines?
2. Scientific evidence on any study which confirms the long-term safety and effectiveness of vaccines?
3. Scientific evidence which proves that any disease reduction at any point in history was directly attributable to vaccination of a population?
4. Scientific justification as to how injecting a human being with a confirmed neurotoxin is beneficial to human health and prevents disease?
5. Scientific justification on how bypassing the respiratory tract or mucous membrane is advantageous and how directly injecting viruses into the bloodstream enhances immune functioning and prevents future infections?
6. Scientific justification on how a vaccine would prevent viruses from mutating?
7. Scientific justification as to how a vaccination can target a virus in an infected individual who does not have the exact viral configuration or strain the vaccine was developed for?

And finally since it is my understanding that vaccines actually place the recipient at risk of developing a wide range of diseases and conditions, you are also required to complete, sign and return the enclosed Liability Statement, in the presence of three witnesses.

Please respond with substance and the requested proofs of claim within seven (7) days, failure to do so will be deemed to mean that no such proofs exist and that it is your medical opinion that the proposed vaccination is **not safe.**

Yours Sincerely,

Liability Statement

I, Dr. **[Doctor's Name]** as the physician administering the **[Name of Vaccine]** vaccine, have thoroughly examined the patient, Mr./Mrs./Miss. **[Your Name]** and have determined that the patient does not have any of the conditions listed below.

I therefore accept full responsibility and full commercial liability should the patient be subsequently diagnosed with any of the following conditions as a result of receiving this vaccine:

[The disease that the vaccine was designed to inoculate against], allergic reactions, ADHD, autism, AIDS, cancer, pneumonia, encephalitis, meningitis, hepatitis, Epstein-Barr disease, encephalopathy, febrile convulsions, non-febrile convulsions, paralytic poliomyelitis and Guillain-Barré syndrome.

Signed in the presence of three witnesses:

Dr. ………………………………………………   Signature ……………………………………………

Date ……………………………………………

Witness ……………………………………………   Signature ……………………………………………

Address ……………………………………………………………………………………………………

………………

Witness ……………………………………………   Signature ……………………………………………

Address ……………………………………………………………………………………………………

………………

Witness ……………………………………………   Signature ……………………………………………

Address ……………………………………………………………………………………………………

………………

The doctor cannot and will not sign the Liability Statement, nor will he provide you with any proof, because there is none. There is not a single double-blind, placebo-controlled study in the history of vaccine development that has ever proven their safety or effectiveness, nor is there any evidence in any country, at any time in history that vaccines have had any direct or consequential effect on the reduction of any type of disease.

In fact, every single study that has ever attempted to prove the safety and effectiveness of vaccines has conclusively established without a shadow of a doubt that they are carcinogenic, mutagenic, neurotoxic or sterilisation agents.

So, why are we being injected with poisonous chemicals and heavy metals in the name of preventing the spread of a so-called disease that would naturally decline anyway?

I don't know, but I will leave it to the reader to decide whether there is a conspiracy by a wealthy, yet psychopathic elite class who believe that there are too many people on the planet and have publically stated time and time again that their goal is to reduce the human population by 90% or more by using, amongst other things, healthcare, sterilisation and vaccines.

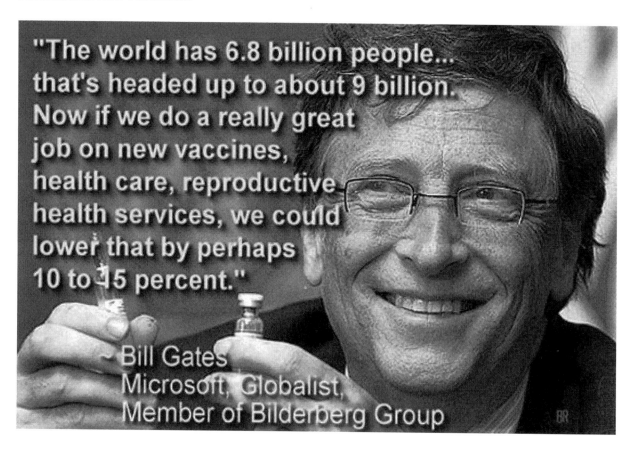

"The world has 6.8 billion people... that's headed up to about 9 billion. Now if we do a really great job on new vaccines, health care, reproductive health services, we could lower that by perhaps 10 to 15 percent."

~ Bill Gates
Microsoft, Globalist,
Member of Bilderberg Group

Death by Doctor

Far more disturbing than the ineffectual nature of medical treatment is the often fatal harm that the treatment inflicts upon its recipients.

In 2003, a group of Medical Doctors and PhD's lead by Gary Null PhD., analyzed and combined all of the published literature in the United States, dealing with injuries and deaths caused by government-protected medicine and published a report entitled "*Death by Medicine*".

The results of this fully referenced report are truly jaw-dropping. It showed that each year 2.2 million people have adverse reactions to properly prescribed pharmaceutical drugs in a hospital setting, 20 million people are prescribed unnecessary antibiotics, 7.5 million people undergo unnecessary medical/surgical procedures, and 8.9 million are hospitalised unnecessarily.

The most stunning statistic, however, is the total number of deaths caused by conventional medicine. Fatalities resulting from medical treatment are known as iatrogenic death or "*Death by Doctor*".

In the United States, iatrogenic damage is now the leading cause of death, ahead of heart disease and cancer.

According to this report, an incredible **783,936** people in the United States fall victim to iatrogenic death each year:

106,000 deaths from properly prescribed pharmaceutical medications

115,000 deaths from bedsores

98,000 deaths from medical errors

199,000 outpatient deaths

108,800 deaths from malnutrition

37,136 deaths from unnecessary procedures

88,000 deaths from Infections

32,000 surgery-related deaths

By contrast, the number of deaths attributable to heart disease in 2001 was **699,697**, while the number of deaths attributable to cancer was **553,252**.

Now, before you join an angry mob and storm the local doctor's surgery, pitchfork in hand, you should know that it is almost certain that these figures are wildly inaccurate.

In his 1994 paper entitled *"Error in Medicine"*, Dr. Lucian L. Leape found that for patients that suffered iatrogenic injury there was a 14% fatality rate and of the three studies he conducted he found a 36%, 20%, and 4% medical error rate.

For some inexplicable reason, Leape chose to use the 4% error rate upon which to base his results, but had he averaged the three rates to 20%, the number of iatrogenic deaths using this average error rate and his 14% fatality rate would actually be 1,189,576.

Using Leape's 1997 medical and drug error rate of 3 million multiplied by the 14% fatality rate he used in 1994 produces an annual death rate of 420,000 for drug errors and medical errors combined. If we accept this number in Dr. Null's report instead of the 106,000 drug errors and 98,000 annual medical errors, this would add another 216,000 deaths, for a total of 999,936 deaths annually.

Even with this staggering conclusion, Leape acknowledged that the sparse data relating to medical errors likely represents only the tip of the iceberg, as only a fraction of medical errors are ever reported.

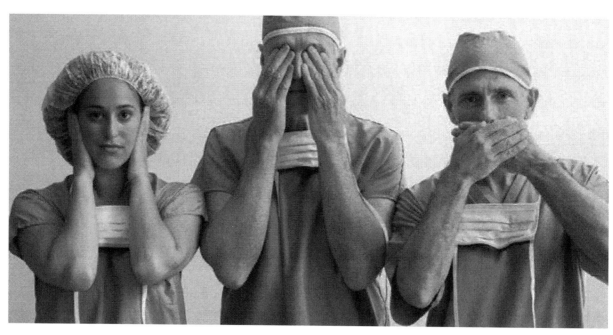

A study conducted in two obstetrical units in the UK found that only about one-quarter of iatrogenic incidents were ever reported, in order to protect staff, preserve reputations, or for fear of reprisals and lawsuits. It appears that all the statistics gathered on iatrogenic damage may substantially underestimate the number of adverse drug and medical therapy incidents. They also suggest that the statistics concerning iatrogenic deaths may be in fact very conservative figures.

Interestingly, when doctors in Los Angeles went on strike for one month in 1976, the number of deaths fell by 18%, similarly, during a doctors strike in Israel in 1983 the mortality rate dropped by a staggering 50%.

It could be said by those of a particularly suspicious nature that rather than a failing, inefficient healthcare system, we have been afflicted with a streamlined and highly efficient public euthanasia system, slowly and quietly culling the old, weak, stupid and undesirable members of society as part of a global eugenics program.

Now might be a good time to get that pitchfork!

* * * *

The claim that medical science has improved the life span of humans is also in question. On June 27th 1930, Royal S. Copeland M.D., a former Health Commissioner for New York, wrote:

> *"Fifty years ago there was a population of a little more than fifty million people, in the United States, 4,000 of whom were centenarians. At the present time, with more than double the population of fifty years ago, there are only 2,841 people who have reached the age of 100."*

If we track the number of centenarians as a percentage of the total population through to the present day the figures would seem to support the medical establishment's claim that it has increased the number of centenarians by more than a factor of ten and, by extension, increased the life spans of the population as a whole.

Year	Centenarians	Total Population	% of Centenarians
1880	4000	50,189,209	0.0079%
1930	2841	123,076,741	0.0023%
1950	2300	152,271,417	0.0015%
1970	106441	205,052,174	0.0052%
1980	10369	227,224,681	0.0046%
1990	37306	249,438,712	0.0149%
2010	53364	310,232,863	0.0172%

But while it seems a rather laudable claim, the figures show that after 130 years of medical practice we have seen a total increase in the number of centenarians of 0.0092%, less than one hundredth of one percent of the population.

Not a terribly impressive performance, yet it is still hailed as a triumph of the medical art by the medical establishment.

However, one thing that is not often taken into account is that 100 years ago, dementia was almost unknown. The centenarian of yesteryear was often fit, healthy and vigorous;

of today's centenarians, fifty percent of them have dementia and sixty to seventy percent are disabled.

Interestingly, if one analyses the 70 year period between 1880 and 1950, the trend is a steady decline in the number of centenarians but then in 1970 the trend suddenly and rather suspiciously reverses with a staggering jump from 2300 centenarians in 1950 to 106,441 a mere twenty years later.

In the 1980 U.S. Department of Commerce publication *"Census of Population: Characteristics of the Population"* it describes how the figure arrived at by the 1980 US Census of 10369 turns out to be double that of the highest independent estimate, and how the figure supplied by the 1970 U.S. Census was given as 106,441 and yet the estimates from ranged from 3,000 to 8,000 and was subsequently revised in a 1976 article in the Journal of the American Statistics Association called *"New Estimates of the Number of Centenarians in the United States"*.   It would therefore appear that such *"official"* figures have been manipulated for public relations purposes and the true number of centenarians is still in decline.   It is worth noting that if one were to use the lowest estimate of 3000 centenarians in 1970 then that would give a percentage of 0.0014% which lies perfectly on the exponential curve of the continuing downward trend.

* * * *

It is clear that the medical establishment knows very little about how to heal the human body and maintain it at optimal health. If one were to follow the scientific and medical proclamations from year to year, it would be a kaleidoscope of confusing contradictions where one year eggs are bad and carbohydrates are good, the following year carbohydrates are bad but polyunsaturated fats are good and then the next, all fats are bad but eggs are good.

It is no wonder that those who put their faith in the white coated puppets have no idea what to believe.

A doctor's head may be filled with facts, figures, interesting anatomical titbits and long made up words in Latin, but if you were to capture one, (probably best accomplished by luring him toward you with a large gin and tonic and a bright, shiny, new carbon fibre sand wedge) pin him in a corner, hold a nine iron to his throat and demand that he tell you everything that he knows about the human body, he would eventually have to admit that he doesn't know a damned thing about how it actually works.

As Carrel, admitted in *"Man, The Unknown"*:

> *"The science of man is still too rudimentary to be useful. – In fact, our ignorance (of the human body) is profound."*

How did we get here?

In 1910, the Rockefeller and the Carnegie foundations commissioned the *"Flexner Report"* to make an inventory of the medical facilities around the United States. At that time there were several different types of medicine, such as Homeopathy, Naturopathy, Chiropractic, Allopathic, Herbalist and Holistic, but following the completion of this report the Rockefeller Foundation massively funded allopathic medicine.

The allopathic approach is a type of medicine that only acts upon a patient's symptoms rather than attempting to repair the cause of them. It is dependent upon drugs, surgery and hospital stays, just perfect for a large corporation like Rockefeller's Standard Oil, who had not only achieved a monopoly in the oil and petroleum industry, but was looking to expand and gain a similar monopoly over fledgling petrochemical and pharmaceutical industries too.

Those allopathic practitioners willing to accept the directions and recommendations of Rockefeller and Carnegie received grants of millions of dollars and drove all other forms of medicine to the margins of a lunatic fringe.

It is interesting to note that according to Dr. Eleanora McBean Ph.D. during the 1918 Spanish flu epidemic, allopathic doctors and hospitals were losing 33% of their patients while non-medical hospitals were healing nearly 100% of cases.

Despite these woeful statistics, allopathic medicine proliferated to the point where today: medical schools only teach allopathy using books about allopathic methods from publishing houses controlled by the same foundations; medical associations (funded and controlled by those same sources) only endorse allopathic medicine; insurance companies only pay out for allopathic methods, which are the only methods that hospitals sanction; and, more importantly for the masses, the only medicine portrayed in the many medical themed television shows shown on television stations dependent on pharmaceutical advertising money or in the similarly controlled Hollywood movies is, surprise surprise, allopathic.

Just to be clear, the allopathic method of treating patients did not achieve its current pre-eminence because of any superior capacity or effectiveness in treating the sick, but was manipulated into place with the application of money and control to create an illusion so real and all-pervasive that this 100 year old pharmacology based method is now perceived to be the only legitimate form of medicine, and it is the traditional, holistic practices that are labelled as *"alternative"* and its practitioners are considered to be *"quacks"* and charlatans practicing witchcraft.

Are Doctors Out To Get Us?

It has to be noted at this point that it is not the doctors themselves that are intentionally harming their patients and, while there are those doctors who are in it for the money, prestige and the social status that has grown up around this invented profession, most became doctors out of a genuine desire to cure diseases and help the sick.

The real culprit here is the training that they received from medical schools that receive funding from the same tax exempt foundations, using books, published through similarly controlled publishing houses, that contain information derived from decades of research funded by the very same sources, all supporting a theory of disease and the idea that the key to *"treating"* these diseases is to mask the symptoms with petrochemical derivatives, or by cutting out the offending or worn out part with very sharp knives.

Doctors, for the most part, are well-meaning individuals who are indoctrinated into a system that leaves them very little scope in their approach to dealing with patients or their symptoms, which isn't much more than look up a patient's list of symptoms in a medical database and prescribe the pharmaceutical drug it recommends.

In the United Kingdom, doctors have quotas to fill and can only allocate eight to ten minutes to a patient which leaves them little option but to deal with patients in this manner.

Doctors in the United States are heavily incentivised by drug companies to dispense particular drugs, with commissions, bonuses and free holidays. They often give free samples of drugs that once a patient starts taking them, it is difficult and/or risky to stop.

Strangely enough, drug dealers in highly addictive narcotics employ exactly the same methods to create their customers. Hmmmmmm...

Sometimes it seems the temptation is just too much. In 2014, Dr. Farid Fata, a prominent cancer doctor in Michigan admitted in court to intentionally and wrongfully diagnosing healthy people with cancer in order to generate highly profitable commissions from the ensuing chemotherapy treatments.

Dr. Fata treated 1,200 patients for which he received $62,000,000 from the government and billed his patients for more than $150,000,000.

What a nice little earner!

The Theory of Disease

The main basis of the allopathic method is the idea that the human body is attacked from outside itself by bacteria and viruses that consume and weaken it causing what are termed *"diseases"*, and it is only with the application of pharmaceutical chemicals and drugs that these diseases can be treated.

At first glance this seems a reasonable hypothesis. After all, we have seen images of bacteria as they swarm and multiply on a microscope slide, and it would seem not to be a good thing to have these beasties growing within us. It would also seem logical that someone with a disease like influenza might sneeze close to us and that we might *"catch"* the same disease by inhaling these viruses and bacteria.

That's how it works in movies and on television isn't it?

However, when one looks at the facts around this theory, it is revealed to be a fanciful construct of circumstantial evidence that falsely interprets the observations, which just happens to be a very lucrative construct that sells a lot of pharmaceutical products

All so-called disease originates from within. We already contain all the bacteria, viruses, Salmonella, E-coli, Candida, Aids, Cancer cells and parasites that we could ever *"catch"*, but normally they lie dormant within us until needed.

The plain fact is that the human body is essentially made of bacteria. There are more bacteria in our bodies than human cells. There are some bacteria which we consider good and others which we are told are bad bacteria. However, there are no such distinctions in the body. Bacteria's main job in the body is to consume dead and dying tissue.

These so-called bad bacteria only become active and multiply when there is dead or dying tissue around to attract them. In the same way, human sanitation workers do not create rubbish, but instead they appear when there is rubbish to deal with. Just like the mold, fungus, bacteria, maggots and parasites, in the environment that we are allegedly separate from, the job of these supposed disease causers is to break down the weak and dead tissue for recycling. If the body is clean and healthy then there is nothing to recycle and they remain dormant.

But, when we consume the highly acidic, meat based diet of the modern world, the body becomes acidic and the meat begins to rot inside us. As a result the parts of our body affected by the acidity and putrefied meat become toxic and weak, and so the dustmen appear to clean them up.

The symptoms we experience are always evidence that the body is healing or eliminating toxins. Our bodies are always dealing with an influx of food that it is continually digesting and toxic substances that it is constantly attempting to eliminate. If our lifestyle is a healthy one and we are limiting and taking care over our food intake, keeping the ingestion of toxins to a minimum and getting plenty of rest then our bodies can keep pace with the amount of work it has to perform. However, there may be times when the body becomes overwhelmed and that is when we experience symptoms – the indication that the body is performing emergency cleansing or healing.

Under normal circumstances, the body's sanitation system works very efficiently. Since we have become accustomed to ingesting acidic foods and meat, the body no longer reacts violently to them. However, when we harbour certain negative thought patterns, a chemical cascade of hormones is released which we experience as an emotion. These chemicals prepare the body to perform any emergency actions that might result from the emotion: some processes are suppressed or shut down altogether; others are activated or over stimulated.

In any case the body is further weakened, especially if this thought pattern is deep seated and persistent, leaving the way clear for particular sanitation workers to proliferate. It is for this reason that the medical misleaders label such viruses and bacteria as *"opportunistic"*.

So-called disease starts as an etheric thought pattern, as invisible and insubstantial as a gas, condenses into the chemicals that evoke a feeling or emotion and materialises in the form of physical symptoms.

One other counter-intuitive point to note is that in order to get sick one must have enough vitality or energy to raise symptoms, for example, the body will create a fever to kill off a viral over-proliferation. However, it takes a considerable amount of energy to create millions of white blood cells or raise the body temperature by five or six degrees. In someone who lacks available energy through gluttony and stress, it is entirely possible that a life threatening condition might not show any symptoms at all.

The allopathic solution to the illusion of disease is a dizzying array of chemical stimulants and suppressants that mask symptoms by poisoning and so deadening the nerves so pain signals are no longer received, and causing an acute toxic reaction such that resources are diverted away from the original problem in order to deal with the more pressing problem presented by the ingested poison. We suppress symptoms thereby suppressing the elimination or healing and turn an acute problem into a chronic one. These new symptoms of elimination are casually dismissed by the white coats as *"side effects,"* when in truth they are the primary and intentional effects as more and more evidence surfaces that most, if not all, of these pharmaceutical toxins are no more efficacious than a sugar pill.

The process of healing cannot be accelerated by any artificial means as it is only the body that can perform healing and the body takes as long as the body takes to do this, but we can aid this process by making as much energy available as possible and assisting in the cleansing effort.

The French philosopher Voltaire once said that:

"The art of Medicine consists of amusing the patient while nature cures the disease"

Repair Procedures

The Tools of the Trade

The tools which we will employ are few and amazingly simple. They are free and almost always available. However, they are incredibly powerful and effective at dealing with any so-called disease. Not because they perform any medical function but because they do not interfere with the body's natural healing processes, rather they aid those processes by providing the necessary energy, assisting with the elimination of toxicity, stimulating and providing information to the immune system, and supplying the body's own life-giving essences to wherever they are most needed.

The following is a brief explanation of the use of distilled water, human urine and fasting as powerful healing modalities.

The Healing Waters

Water is an amazing substance that we know very little about. Not only is it the most powerful known solvent, it has the highest surface tension of any liquid, it is also the only substance that can exist in three states simultaneously, liquid, solid and gaseous. It is also unique in that, out of all the substances on earth, water is the only one that expands when it freezes and contracts when heated.

Another peculiar characteristic of water is that it can be structured by human emotions and intention.

Dr. Masaru Emoto took identical bottles of water and on one he wrote, *"I love you"* and on another he wrote, *"You make me sick."* After a period he took a sample of each, flash froze them and studied the patterns.

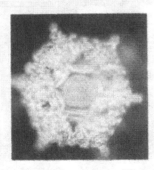  

"I love you."   "You make me sick."   "Thank you."

He found that the water imprinted with messages of love froze into beautiful geometric patterns and that the water impregnated with negative emotions were randomised, unstructured, *"ugly"* patterns. Somehow the water had taken on the intent expressed by the words attached to them.

Dr. Emoto's Rice Experiment involves two identical jars of rice soaked in water with the message *"I love you"* written upon one jar and *"I hate you"* on the other. The jars are placed next to each other on a window sill and inspected after several weeks. Amazingly, time after time, the rice with positive message still appears fresh while the jar labelled with the negative message is foul and rotten.

Dr. Emoto's Rice Experiment

A brief internet search on *"Emoto Rice Experiment"* will show that this experiment has been performed thousands of times by ordinary people sharing their experiences on the internet all with the same results.

Water has a memory and is structured by experience. The human body is mostly water with a few impurities, that is structured by a lifetime of experiences. The planet earth is mostly water, with a few impurities and is structured by a whole world of experiences over billions of years. And since Hydrogen is the most abundant element in the universe and Oxygen is formed as a product of stellar explosions so it would appear that the whole universe is mostly water with a few impurities, structured by universal experience.

As above, so below, ad infinitum.

Distilled Water

Nature only ever creates distilled water. All forms of precipitation are distilled, as are the waters that form the juice within fruits and the water in human urine. As the sun heats up the sea, the water evaporates, and rises high into the atmosphere where it meets the cooler air and condenses into clouds of water vapour. When these clouds reach a certain density threshold the vapour forms droplets of pure water purified by this process of steam distillation.

The human body performs a body temperature type of distillation as blood passes through tiny tubules called *"nephrons"* in the kidneys to form the distilled water component of urine and it is thought that a similar process is at work within fruit trees as they form their fruit.

The only man made distilled water is created using the process of steam distillation, which boils and subsequently condenses the steam and passes the distillate through a carbon filter to capture any foreign substances that happen to have a lower boiling point than water.

Filtered water is not the same as distilled as even the most efficient reverse osmosis filter might produce water with 70 – 100ppm (parts per million) of dissolved solids, steam distilled water contains 0ppm.

Counter top distillers, like the one shown here, are commercially available for home use at fairly reasonable prices.

The medical establishment will tell you not to drink distilled water because it will leach minerals out of your body, giving you the impression that the calcium will be sucked out of your bones, which are then likely to snap like twigs in the slightest of breezes. But like a great many things proclaimed by the wise and all-knowing medical industry, it is only half true but completely misleading.

What they fail to mention is that there are two types of minerals. There are Organic, or living, minerals that your body uses, like the living calcium in your bones and teeth, and living iron in your blood. But there is another form that these minerals exist in and that is inorganic, which is essentially dead matter, rock or dirt. Mineral water, spring water and tap water all contain these inorganic forms and despite the advertising hype, the human body cannot metabolise them, so they are absorbed into the body and lodge themselves within various tissues and organs.

When these inorganic minerals collect in the spaces between the cartilage of the joints, the white coats call this arthritis. When they collect in and calcify the arterial walls of blood vessels the resultant symptoms are known as arteriosclerosis, leading to heart disease and strokes, and when they collect in the eyes, this is known as glaucoma or cataracts. They are also responsible for gall stones, kidney stones and a whole range of, what the allopaths call, *"diseases"*.

Distilled water does indeed leach minerals out of the body. However, it only dissolves and washes away inorganic minerals while it leaves organic minerals untouched. We, of course, know this intuitively since we use water to dissolve dirt (inorganic minerals) when we wash our clothes. The dirt stays in the water, but water alone will not shift organic substances such as blood, sweat and grass stains.

Part of the confusion around distilled water stems from use of the word *"distilled,"* which sounds very daunting and clinical and conjures up images of a laboratory or industrial process. However, to put it into perspective, another way of saying *"distilled"*, is *"pure"*. It then becomes difficult to take seriously anyone who suggests that pure water is harmful.

Distilled water is very helpful in aiding the human body to cleanse itself, but the body naturally produces its own form of distilled water which is far more effective and beneficial.

Now Wash Your Hands

The human body produces its own distilled water remedy, which is always available, costs nothing and is the perfect remedy for all known maladies. It is a remedy that has been known and used for over 5,000 years but over the last seventy or eighty years has fallen out of favour, or rather has been suppressed, by an industry that makes literally trillions of dollars a year keeping people sick and dependent on symptom suppressants. If this remedy were known by the masses then the pharmaceutical industry would cease to exist overnight. As such, a social taboo has been created against this practice bolstered by subtle programming by the mass media, as well as half truths and downright lies from the medical mafia.

The remedy, if you haven't already guessed, is **urine**. The medical establishment is more than happy to let you believe that urine is nothing more than a waste product. The media arm of their cartel will reinforce this myth with subtle cues that keep you afraid of coming into contact with this dirty, disgusting substance but, as you will see, this is simply to keep the pharmaceutical arm of the cartel selling your their worthless poisons.

Urine is literally your life blood.

When a doctor takes a blood sample and stands it up in a test tube, the red blood cells sink to the bottom of the tube, leaving a yellow liquid at the top, your blood plasma. This is your urine. In fact the medical term for urine is *"plasma ultrafiltrate"*, that is, ultra-filtered blood plasma.

As your blood circulates it transports oxygen to all the cells of the body, provides necessary chemical stimulation to the organs and carries away the toxic waste products from the organs and cell deterioration. The blood goes to the liver which filters out all the waste, the viruses and pathogens. The now purified blood then passes to the kidneys, which are not designed to screen out waste but to keep the blood in balance by regulating the proportions of the blood's vital life giving necessities, because having too much of any of these critical substances is just as bad as having not enough. This excess is stored in the bladder where the body can reabsorb some of these components if there is immediate need; otherwise the rest is flushed away as urine.

Urine is literally a snapshot of everything your body needs at that moment. It is composed of hundreds of beneficial substances such as uric acid, urea, creatinine and hippuric acid, sodium chloride, sulphates, phosphates, sodium, oxalic acid, alcohol, enzymes, antibodies and hormones.

The following is the composition of the average daily urine output:

Allantion	25-30 g	**Iron**	0.5 mg
Alanine	38 mg	**Lysine**	56 mg
Arginine	32 mg	**Magnesium**	100 mg
Ascorbic acid	30 mg	**Manganese**	0.5 mg
Allantoin	12 mg	**Methionine**	10 mg
Amino acids	2.1 g	**Nitrogen**	15 g
Bicarbonate	140 mg	**Ornithine**	10 mg
Biotin	35 mg	**Pantothenic acid**	3 mg
Calcium	23 mg	**Phenylalanine**	21 mg
Creatinine	1.4 mg	**Phosphorus**	9 mg
Cystine	120 mg	**Potassium**	2.5 mg
Dopamine	0.40 mg	**Proteins**	5 mg
Epinephrine	0.01 mg	**Riboflavin**	0.9 mg
Folic acid	4 mg	**Tryptophan**	28 mg
Glucose	100 mg	**Tyrosine**	50 mg
Glutamic acid	308 mg	**Urea**	24.5 mg
Glycine	455 mg	**Vitamin B6**	100 mg
Inositol	14 mg	**Vitamin B12**	0.03 mg
Iodine	0.25 mg	**Zinc**	1.4 mg

These substances are pre-digested and so are immediately available for use by the body, in exactly the right proportions and containing all the information to restore your body to optimum performance and help recovery from so-called incurable and deadly diseases.

Contrary to what we have been taught and conditioned to believe, urine is clean and sterile, is a natural antiseptic, a disinfectant, an antihistamine, an anti-inflammatory, an anti bacterial and antiviral agent. It contains antibodies and antigens that can trigger or calm immune responses. It stimulates the body's organs and tissues to release toxins, and it is packed with stem cells, embryonic cells that can become anything and literally roam around the body looking for things to repair.

Urine is an amazing elixir of life and health, it holds a complete blueprint of the body's current condition, and contains antibodies and antigens that provide detailed information to body's immune system, helping to prevent allergies and stopping asthma attacks.

Ingesting urine allows the body to recycle valuable substances vital to its wellbeing and also liberates a great deal of energy for use in repair and maintenance operations simply because it supplies the body with instant access to vital substances without the very energy intensive overhead of having the organs and glands reproduce the substances.

Urine helps the body to heal from illness by dissolving the waste products and accumulated toxins in the body by stimulating the organs and tissues to eliminate them from the body through the mouth, nose, anus or skin. Because of this process there may be vomiting, cough, mucus, diarrhoea or skin eruptions. These are known as detoxification symptoms, and as with all other symptoms, they are a necessary step in healing the illness, and will usually disappear automatically within a few days.

Urine has been proved in countless cases to rebuild damaged vital organs and tissues of the lungs, pancreas, liver, brain, heart etc. Its amazing disinfectant and antiseptic properties mean that urine provides effective healing for injuries, burns and skin diseases. When used externally, urine stimulates the skin to eliminate toxins also. Most people have heard that urine is very effective in drawing out the venom of a poisonous jellyfish sting, however it is not just jellyfish venom that urine helps the skin to eliminate, but all toxins.

Since urine contains most of the blood factors essential to the repair of human tissue, wounds, burns and skin irritations respond miraculously to its application, bleeding stops immediately, pain disappears and the affected part heals quickly.

Urine is not therefore, a medicine for any particular disease, but it is a complete remedy for total health.

Less is More

Fasting is the practice of not eating or drinking anything except liquids such as urine, distilled water or freshly squeezed fruit juice. Although, strictly speaking it is liquid fast, it is one of the most effective methods of dealing with any kind of illness or disease.

Whenever we become ill, our intuitive reaction is that we do not feel like eating, but then the *"common sense"* logic, instilled in us by well-meaning parents, kicks in and we eat *"to keep our strength up"*.

Our amazingly intelligent body knows what to do and yet we ignore or misinterpret the message it sends us and sabotage its attempts to heal itself by robbing it of the energy it requires to accomplish the task.

Fasting is an effective and powerful healing modality; it literally redistributes the body's energy by resting the digestive system so that the energy that it would normally be using can be reallocated to repair and maintenance of the body's systems. When we stop eating, our body redirects its energy towards eliminating the toxins and waste stored in our tissues and cells. The extra energy also provides a boost to the immune and repair systems such that disease, parasites, cysts, tumours and lumps will be attacked by it as well as being starved of the chemical stimulation that the food would have supplied.

Common sense would dictate though that if you fasted for any significant length of time then the body will lose lots of weight by consuming its own muscle and body fat, leaving it weak and skeletal. In most cases the body does indeed lose weight and become weak but it does so due to its level of toxicity, a condition known as autointoxication.

During a fast the body begins to liberate internal toxins which cause the decomposition of body protein and fat, and as the body's eliminatory systems receive an energy boost, greater amounts of the body's toxins are excreted through the bowels, the skin and the breath. It is not unusual for a person who is fasting to experience weight loss, a loss of vitality as well as terrible body odour, bad breath and poor skin condition. However, if the body were sufficiently clean and free of toxicity, there would be no condition of autointoxication and no weight loss would occur.

Essentially, you lose weight on a fast because you're full of crap.

Breatharianism

Professor Hilton Hotema, in his book Man's Higher Consciousness described how man has fallen from the perfect state of Breatharianism through various stages and at every stage, each new habit we fell into, our bodies had to adapt to the new toxic habit, and just like Claude Bernard's sparrow, we lost a measure of our vitality, our susceptibility to what is called disease increased and our lifespans decreased. However, I would suggest that we, in the modern era, have fallen through more stages than Hotema could have envisaged.

1. Breatharian
2. Liquidarian
3. Fruitarian
4. Vegetarian
5. Carnivore
6. **Burned Omnivore**
7. **Chemovore**

The last two stages reflect our current relationship with our food. Our current diet, at first glance could be regarded as that of a Burned Omnivore as most people eat a combination of meat, fruit and vegetables that have been treated in some fashion by the habit of cooking.

No other animal on earth requires its food to be cooked, and when one takes a step back and looks at this practice objectively, it is difficult to imagine why we would develop such a habit. Some might argue that most root vegetables are almost impossible to digest without cooking to break down the cellulose and starch, but that would suggest that we are not meant to be eating root vegetables in the first place.

Fortunately we can gauge how much of an affinity the body has for cooked food by its reaction to it.

When the body encounters an irritant, a poison or a dangerous foreign organism or substance, it responds by producing white blood cells, which the fraudsters in white coats call leukocytes, in sufficient quantities to attack, overwhelm or envelop the source of the problem. The medical circus performers have a fancy name for this process too, they call it *"leukocytosis"*, and they will tell you that whenever the body goes into leukocytosis, it is always in response to a poisonous or otherwise dangerous substance or an infection. EXCEPT in the case of cooked food, where they call it *"Digestive Leukocytosis"* and that, apparently, is just fine and dandy...

"Nothing to see here, just keep eating the bacon sandwiches."

The human body reacts to cooked food as if it were a poisonous substance, but, strangely enough, if the same foodstuffs are ingested in their raw form the body does not produce leukocytes to combat them.

Hmmmm, interesting...

The culprit, in this case, is likely to be a substance called acrylamide that forms in foods during the cooking process. Acrylamide is highly carcinogenic and is found to be present in almost all cooked foods.

Even more worryingly, the last few decades have seen an increase in chemical *"Non-Foods"* produced by huge global corporations which no longer deal with whole foods, rather they derive chemical and textural traits from natural and genetically modified and pesticide laden fruits and vegetables. Chemicals, textures and colourings are mixed and matched to create highly addictive food-like substances at the cheapest possible cost in order to maximise their profits.

At the time of writing, the average diet consists of mainly processed chemical *"non-foods"* which provide no benefit to the human body and progressively poisons it. Over time the body responds to the accumulation of toxins with, what the medical establishment calls, *"old age"* and *"disease"*. The vast majority of people are unaware that they are dying of what they eat, because it does not immediately affect them and so they rarely make the connection is between their favourite snack and the heart disease, diabetes or cancer that develops later in life.

As previously shown, the human body does not require food for its survival, and by working one's way back up Hotema's stages of decline to less and less dense foodstuffs while simultaneously reducing portion sizes, the body can be slowly weaned off food altogether.

Now, I am not suggesting that everyone should immediately turn breatharian and stop eating altogether. We all addicted to eating, but I hope that you have begun to see that the human body does not actually require food and that fasting is a powerful healing modality because it frees up an enormous amount of energy for use in healing the body.

As a breatharian, living in the high places where the air was pure, the human body was a closed loop eco-system that, apart from the breath of life, required no input and emitted no output. When we began to introduce food into the body, not only do we rob the body of its energy in the digestive process, but it now has to eliminate all the physical matter as well as deal with the overproduction of hormones, enzymes, minerals, vitamins and proteins etc. stimulated by the presence of the food and its chemical components and thus the body operates at much less than its optimum capacity, under a certain amount of chronic stress and has to defecate to eliminate waste and urinate to remove excess blood products. All at the cost of its longevity, and the denser the food source the greater the trade off in life span.

At this point in time, we are addicted to food, but the point to remember is that there is a huge difference between eating for pleasure and eating because you believe you cannot survive without it.

From this new perspective, you can reduce your intake of food without the fear of starvation and simultaneously provide your body with an abundance of energy for healing and prevention of disease.

As previously noted, the further up Hotema's list you go, the less dense the foodstuff becomes, so if you currently eat meat then you might start making a habit of fasting two days out of the week and after two months, move up to vegetarian and after two months progress to eating only fruit and fasting a week every month. After 8 months you can progress to the liquidarian stage where you would consume only distilled liquids, in other words, pure water, freshly squeezed fruit juice and your own urine.

The aim is not to become a breatharian as such, but a liquidarian that sometimes eats fruit and very occasionally fresh vegetables for pleasure.

The advantage of this approach is that we will begin to reverse the trade off and regain some of the benefits of breatharianism, without having to give up eating altogether. The body's energy levels will increase dramatically, there will be an increased resistance to so-called disease, the signs of so-called *"old age"* will begin to reverse and we may well see a greatly increased life span.

Operating Your Body

The Meaning of Life in 30 Seconds

Our culture proposes that the entire point of our lives is to go to school, do well in exams to go on to higher education so that we can get a really good job working really hard in order to afford to buy enough material stuff, to attract a mate of sufficient quality so that we pass on the best genetic mix to our progeny. We work even harder so that we can amass lots more material stuff and gain status over our peers until we retire (if we make it to retirement age, which is carefully selected so that the majority of people never reach it and claim the pension they have been saving for most of their lives) by which time we are too old to live the life we were working toward anyway, and finally we die hoping that we were successful in passing on our values to our children so they get to be even better at repeating the whole process again ad nauseam.

Ok, 37 seconds then.

Is that really the best we can think of as the meaning and purpose of our lives?

We are experiencing beings, and creators of our experience. We are a finite expression of an infinite universal consciousness looking at itself from countless different viewpoints and perspectives, to figure out what it means to be. Our purpose here is to experience all there is to experience, and all experience is valid, there is no such thing as good and bad, these are merely human labels on varying degrees of experience.

The physicist Tom Campbell described it best.

Imagine the infinite, universal consciousness or God creating a beautiful ocean but the in order to know what it feels like, God might create a big toe to dip into it. Now, the big toe's job is simply to experience so that the toe's owner knows what it feels like, it. It doesn't matter if the water is too cold, too hot or not water at all but corrosive hydrochloric acid, the experience is valid no matter what it is.

Unlike a big toe, however, we have been given a certain amount of free will and the power to create and shape our own experience and in that respect, our lives are like that of *"Truman"* in the 1998 film *"The Truman Show"*.

In The Truman Show, Jim Carrey plays Truman, a man who was sold as a child to a television corporation and placed on an island *"habitat"* surrounded by actors inside a 50 mile wide dome. Truman believes he is living a normal life; however the drama of his life is being scripted by a director, played out by actors and watched by millions on *"The Truman Show"*.

There are many things that are on the edge of Truman's consciousness but do not actually exist within his finite universe inside the dome. Truman might have seen people hang gliding on television, for instance, or he might have seen it in a magazine. One way or another Truman will have on the edge of his consciousness the possibility that a man can strap himself into a big kite and fly around, but it literally does not exist in his universe, until he focuses his attention on it.

If Truman were to suddenly decide that he wants to try hang-gliding, then the director suddenly has to find a couple of actors who know how to teach hang-gliding, create a hang-gliding club or two, populated by more actors, add a shop in a remote part of town so that Truman can buy equipment, perhaps even have part of the island landscaped and the wind patterns changed to make a good hang gliding experience, so that when Truman acts upon his intentions his universe has expanded in that direction so he can have the experience he intends. In other words particulate reality has been condensed from waves of infinite possibilities by an Observer/Experiencer/Creator.

There are many things on the edge of your consciousness that do not exist in your universe, such as starving children in Africa. You may have seen horrifying images on television, read about their plight in newspapers or heard songs written to raise funds to aid them but in the same way that Schrödinger's cat was neither alive or dead, until you go and see for yourself, they only exist in a state of quantum uncertainty, a possibility amongst waves of infinite possibilities until you look and collapse that wave into particulate reality, so that now you can experience starving children in Africa. Your universe expands in that direction and so your adventure continues.

This is why we will never find the edge of our universe or the smallest constituent of matter, the further we look the more that we will create to see.

We experience this characteristic of simultaneous creation and perception all the time in our daily lives but rarely acknowledge it as significant.

Imagine that you want to buy a car, and you have decided on a red Ford Fiesta, the first thing that will happen is that you start seeing red Ford Fiestas everywhere. Most will assume that they are merely paying more attention to red Fiestas than before and nothing particularly strange is going on, but the fact is that before you decided what you wanted to buy, the probability that red Ford Fiestas would appear to you was statistically exactly the same as any other car, but once you had made your decision, it was the actual statistical probability of encountering red Ford Fiestas that increased.

This phenomenon has been proven in experiments with random number generators that produce a random stream of ones and zeros which always works out to roughly fifty percent ones and fifty percent zeros. A random number generator was started and an experienced meditator was asked to concentrate on producing more ones than zeros and when the output was checked, indeed there were many more ones than chance would dictate.

Further experiments proved the quantum uncertainty aspect, by recording a random number generator sequence and sealing the results in an envelope unseen, they again asked a meditator to concentrate on producing more zeros than ones in a sequence that has already taken place and the result was significantly more zeros than ones.

The only real difference between our *"reality"* and Truman's is not only are we the star of the show, we are also the audience, the director, the producer, the writer, the set designer, and all the other actors. We are like a child who has made a stage out of an old shoebox and has made some cardboard cut-out characters to play with and is acting out scenarios from his imagination.

Truman discovering that his reality is not as he believed it to be.

This reality is a game, a story, like a multiplayer first person video game. For the character on screen, your avatar, everything feels real. It bumps into walls, it can be damaged or hurt, but the truth is that the whole world your avatar is *"experiencing"* is being generated just for that character and for YOU, the one seeing through your avatar's eyes, and even though it seems like there are other people there with you, there aren't. It's a multi-player game but the other players are just characters in your universe. Everyone else is in their own universe, their computers are generating their own separate universe and even though their avatars interact with your universe, they do not exist in it, only you do.

You are what your whole universe is doing. It's all about you, it's your story and you are simultaneously writing it and acting that story out as you go along in a 3D Technicolor,

Surround Sound, fully interactive life simulator where you can do anything, be anyone and try out anything you want. It feels very real, it has to feel real otherwise there's no danger, there's no fun.

So to challenge our previous record of 37 seconds we can sum up the meaning of life as:

"The true meaning of being is to truly be" - Allegedly Dave

4.2 seconds – that's a new state record.

Operating the Universe

The Hermetic philosophy of the Egyptian alchemist Thoth, tells of the principle of correspondence, summarised to the well known phrase:

"As above so below, as below so above".

This principle is represented in modern times by the concept of Fractal Mathematics.

A Fractal is essentially a simple rule iterated an infinite number of times that gives rise to infinite complexity, and yet each level of magnification remains similar to all other levels, meaning that one can zoom in or out to any extent and the pattern will be similar to all other views and zoom levels.

A computer rendering of the Mandlebrot Set fractal

Interestingly, it appears that the physical universe that we appear to inhabit is structured as a fractal, that is, it is self similar at all levels of magnification.

A section of coastline hundreds of miles long as viewed from a satellite, is indistinguishable from a smaller section a mile long as well as the microscopic edge of one of the grains of sand on that coast and undoubtedly if one were able to zoom out from the Earth, the edge of the galactic structure within which the Earth is embedded would also appear similar.

The physical world was manifested out of an incomprehensible mental plane by an infinite mind that is unimaginable to us, but according to this principle and the self similarity at all levels of the physical realm, there is a correspondence or a harmony between the two – the incomprehensible and the mundane. Our world is a reflection of the realm beyond the physical, our minds are an echo of the infinite living mind.

I mentioned earlier how our reality is like a first person video game, where the game is viewed through the eyes of the onscreen character. This is not a surprising concept if we accept the principle of *"as above so below, as below as above"*. It follows that the realm above the level of reality would express a resonance at this level.

In a typical first person view video game, before the actual game starts, the player selects the physical characteristics of his avatar and often goes on to choose it's personality traits, such as skill, bravery and intelligence.

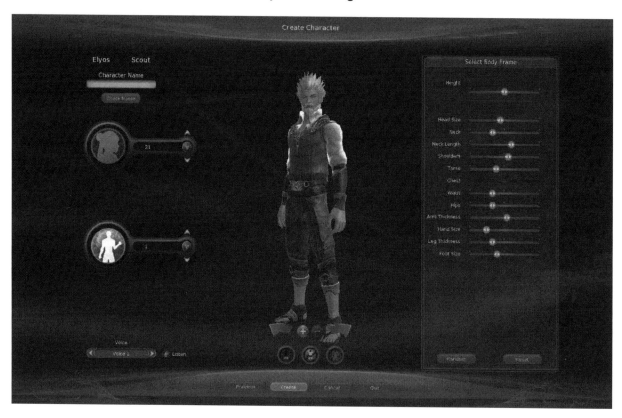

Video game character creation screen

Once the avatar is fully defined, the player chooses the mission and the game starts. The avatar manifests into a world which appears very real to it. It appears to have three dimensional space, time seems to pass, there are objects that are apparently solid and there seems to be rules that cannot be broken or transcended but from player's point of view the world that the avatar inhabits is merely a construction of light pixels with no real concept of time as he can pause the game or go back *"in time"* and play an earlier saved game. The first person video game is an echo of the realm that the human body inhabits.

From the perspective of the body it exists in three dimensional space and time surrounded by what appears to be separate and unconnected objects, and just like the teenager who plays video games to experience what it is like to be a fighter pilot or Formula One race driver or even an Elf in a Lord of the Rings adventure, the human body is a means by which a disembodied spirit can experience adventures on Earth. But just as everything in the video game is made from the same stuff, that is, an organised mass of light pixels and information, so too is reality is made up of a mass of conscious waves of energy structured and organised by information.

When the *"mission"* starts within these experiential video games, the avatar appears to have free will, it can seemingly go where it likes and do whatever it wants, however eventually it will inevitably arrive at a point known as a *"cut-scene"*, where game play is halted and a predetermined sequence plays out to advance the story.

If the player *"goes with the flow"* of events, following the signs and hints left by the game designer, then the avatar arrives at its predetermined milestone having experienced all the interesting plot points, but should the player decide to exercise his free will and go against the flow then his journey will be fraught with difficulties and resistance, problematic circumstances, blind alleyways, frustrating dead-end situations which will still nonetheless grind the avatar towards the cut-scene having missed the points of interest that were laid out for it to experience.

A human life appears to operate in the same manner; before we are born it seems that certain way-points are set out for us, to advance our own stories and if we follow the trail of intuition, serendipity, and the things that keep us in a blissful, excited state then we flow with the river of events that sweep us on to the next way-point over and around any obstacles via the most scenic route.   However, we always have the option to choose a path that pits us against the current, in which case our life journey will be a frustrating struggle against the inevitable arrival at a point that is likely not to make much sense to one who has failed to notice the flow, meaning and direction of their life.

Thoughts become things

The idea of the video game symbolising our three dimensional reality is an astoundingly powerful metaphor, and a metaphor is not just a linguistic construct, it is the fundamental way that we interact with this reality construct. When you peel back the illusion of reality, everything is mind, intent, metaphor and manifestation.

Imagine that you decide to make a chair. As soon as you have the idea, it **will** manifest into reality, whether **you** build it or not. If you design something in your imagination, it becomes part of the *"cosmic internet"* (or it was already there and you picked up on it) the sum total of human experience that everyone has access to, and if not you, then someone else will bring it into reality.

But let's say that you really want to make this chair, what actually happens is that you imagine a set of information and intentions, which we call a *"design"*. Your consciousness then moves what you perceive to be your hands, which are really part of the energy field that you believe is part of you and that you have learned to exercise full control over. Your *"hands"* manipulate intention imprinted patterns of the energy field which you perceive as *"tools"* that you don't believe you have direct control over, (which, of course, you do because you are, through the metaphor of hands). Your consciousness uses these *"tools"* to restructure another part of the energy field with a vibrational frequency that you recognise as wood, until it matches your design and, voila, you have what you perceive to be a chair. But in reality, it is a standing wave of conscious energy structured with intention and information that match your design.

If you had a different metaphor that involved materialising objects from thin air, then the chair would have simply appeared out of nowhere (though probably with a weird Swedish name, flat packed, with no instructions and a few screws missing).

In order to manifest or alter reality on this plane of existence, it would appear that we must use higher laws to manipulate the lower laws of reality and we do this using metaphor and symbolism.

One very powerful metaphor is known as the placebo effect: the astounding phenomenon where if a sick person is given a dummy medicine or procedure that has no effects of any kind but yet utterly believes that it will cure them then that person will manifest a cure.

Another powerful metaphor uses visual symbolism directly.

"Sigil Magic" involves creating a sigil, a meaningless looking symbol designed from the  unique letters from the words of a written intention. The intent is embedded in the sigil and so, when the *"magician"*, or anyone else fixes their attention upon it, then the intent is manifest into reality.

The British Standards logo, shown here, is clearly a sigil. You can see that it incorporates a 'B' and 'S' that would suggest that it represents the words "British Standards" however, there also appears to be a 'V' embedded within it, so the intent imprinted into this sigil may be more than we might believe.

Once again, knowing the non-physical, intention driven nature of the universe, and the power of focused attention, sigil magic may not seem too farfetched.

The modern culture is saturated with sigils disguised as corporate logos to draw our attention and exert a psychological and energetic influence upon the mass of humanity who worship them.

The ancient peoples of the world knew the power of metaphor and symbolism to create miraculous effects. However, this information has been excised from the indigenous peoples and concentrated in secret societies that have hoarded this esoteric information.

The members of these secret societies, who are positioned in government, media and the multi-national corporations, certainly know the power of metaphor and symbolism because they use it against us all the time to magically make us think and act in the way they wish us to.

Modern sigils - more than meets the eye

Life and How to Play It

In his book, *"The Biology of Belief"*, Dr. Bruce Lipton shows how our personal beliefs and attitudes actually changes our DNA and, therefore, our internal and external biology. However, many astounding experiments have shown that these same beliefs actually shape our reality around us.

In one such experiment, named the *"Phantom DNA Experiment"*, Russian scientists P.P. Gariaev and V.P. Poponin demonstrated that the presence of human DNA affects and structures photons of light as they randomly pop in and out of existence and that even when the DNA is removed, the photons remain aligned to the space the DNA previously inhabited. This means that our DNA influences the structure of space in some manner that affects the building blocks of our physical universe... And we control that DNA with our beliefs and intent.

Cool!

The problem is that we cannot make use of this incredible ability without a great deal of effort and practice as 99.8% of the time we are operating from subconscious programming we received almost from birth.

During the first six years of our lives, we are implanted with all of our fundamental beliefs about ourselves and the reality we inhabit and overwhelmingly those beliefs are negative and about limitations.

We are not taught that we are immensely powerful, spiritual beings, one with all that is, operating an amazing, self repairing *"Earth Rover"*, capable of creating and shaping the physical reality it inhabits. Instead we are repeated told that we are small, insignificant and imperfect creatures that arrived here because of a series of accidents. These bodies, which encompass the whole of our being, are badly designed, prone to failures, subject to wear and tear and utterly dependent on experts to keep them running.

According to a Western culture that is increasingly being foisted upon the rest of the world, we have no individual power to affect our world. Rather we are at the mercy of powerful forces and powerful rulers, and our only purpose in this life is the collection and consumption of material goods, available only if we work, for most of our active lives, to collect certain pieces of paper supplied by a certain family business.

The subconscious mind is the habit mind. So long as this part of our mind is in control of our day to day existence the latter view of the universe and our place in it will remain dominant. In order to take full control of your body and your universe, harken to the words of Yoda, the wise and powerful green sock puppet.

"You must unlearn what you have learned"

Here are a few tips to help you operate your universe:

Take time to Meditate.

Sit comfortably, close your eyes and just be, notice any thoughts that might come up and just let them go by without dwelling or focusing upon them, or alternatively, focus on a bright point of light for a few seconds, close your eyes and concentrate on the image of the light behind your closed eyelids, try and make it glow brighter and stronger. Meditate for 20 minutes each day.

This will seem difficult at first but with practice it will become easier as you mental focus and clarity improves.

If, however you cannot seem to find 20 minutes in your day to meditate, then this is a clear indication that you should meditate for **40 minutes** a day.

Be present wherever you are.

Be mindful of the present moment.

When you are replaying, in your head, the past or worrying about the future then your subconscious programming is in charge of your actions and mental/physical state in the now.

Watch for negative thoughts, quiet them and teach the subconscious mind new thought patterns that better serve you.

Remember that this is a game.

This is a game that YOU have chosen to come here and play. So no matter what situation that your character and body finds itself in, whether ecstatic or dreadful, YOU, the player, are in absolute bliss.

Even death is not a bad thing; it may be the end of the particular character YOU are playing, but YOU will always exist, because YOU have always existed. The life and death of your avatar is not only vitally important as *"what the universe is doing"* but simultaneously it is as inconsequential as an individual cell in your body.

Pain, strife and suffering are all part of the game. No game is worth playing if it's all ladders and no snakes, there have to be challenges, obstacles to overcome to make the game interesting but always remember that heaven and hell are both right here and right now. You are the deciding factor.

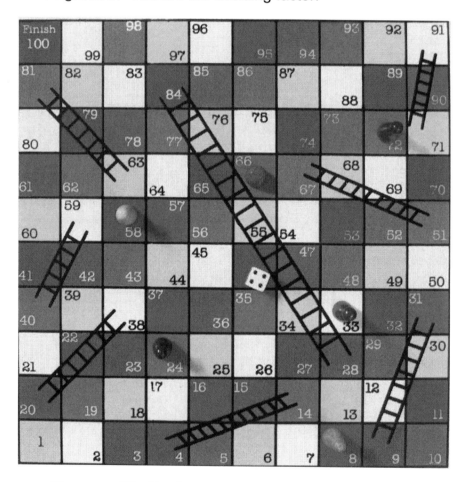

The game of "Ladders" - not so much fun without the challenge.

Just like the Mars Rover, rolling around the surface of another planet under the control of an operator at NASA, your body is an *"Earth Rover"*, it is the only way for YOU, as a disembodied spirit to experience love, grief, anger, chocolate, a sunset or a rainbow.

It is a privilege to be here, and every experience is valid and equally important, so even if you live for a second, you have already won.

Remember the rules of this game and play consciously

There appear to be two rules that govern the human experience of this universe and they are: whatever you put out into it, comes back to you multiplied; and what you fail to learn will be repeated over and over until you do.

Knowing these rules allows the character that you are playing to stay in harmony with the universe and true to that character's purpose. However, there is a way to consciously take control of your experience.

Whatever experience you would like to have, you can explicitly ask the universe to provide it. Unfortunately the universe does not speak English, French or Swahili. It does, however, speak the language of emotion and intent.

The first step is to visualise that experience in minute detail. If you have to cut out pictures from magazines, draw it, make models, make music, then do whatever you need to do to crystallise that experience in your mind. But along with that vision, feel what it is like to have that experience, spend time everyday feeling how it feels to be that person having that experience right now and feel gratitude because the universe has already created that experience for you right now. You may not be able to see it but it already exists, just like when a sculptor has a clear vision of the statue he is about to carve from the solid block of marble before him, the beautiful statue already exists inside the marble block.

Once the intent and feeling are clearly defined and acknowledged to exist right now then let it go, confident in the knowledge that it already exists and it will find you.

Remember, you are a creator in this universe. When you have focused your intent and feeling upon something then you have already brought it into being.

Enjoy playing!

This place, the Earth, is a sandbox, one of an infinite number of different sandboxes, constructed for you to play in.

Nothing is serious here because nothing your character can do here is permanent, no matter what you do, what structures that you build, in a thousand years or ten thousand years there will remain no trace of your avatar or its deeds. Your avatar is born into this world with nothing, nothing it does is of any consequence whatsoever and after a time, it leaves this place with nothing. You are here to play, view life from your unique perspective, learn from it and enjoy the experience.

Don't try to hang on to things that you have become attached to. To paraphrase Princess Leia in the film "*Star Wars*":

> *"The more you tighten your grip on it, the more it will slip through your fingers."*

This is true for money, material possessions, circumstances and relationships. Everything is transient, everything is in motion and the only constant you can be certain of, is change (and that England will always lose against Germany in the World Cup). Even if you are in the most wonderful relationship with the most perfect soul mate, you cannot hold on to it forever. Both you and your soul mate will die at some point, whether it is in a month from now, a year or in fifty years, and in the meantime an infinite number of circumstances and scenarios can play out to bring it to a close. Change is the very essence of life.

So enjoy and be thankful for the experience of where you happen to be in the NOW, because the HERE and NOW is all there is.

You are here… Always!

Follow your passion

Human society exists to distract you away from being who you are meant to be. You have a purpose in this life, but if you get caught up in those things that society tells us that you have to do, then you will likely miss it.

Find out what excites you, what is it that you would gladly spend all your free time doing without any kind of reward. This step might take some time to accomplish.

When you find what that is, then do it, without any regard for the consequences. Follow your heart and watch the obstacles, even seemingly impossible ones move out of your way.

Watch for synchronicities, those amazing so-called coincidences that point your way to the next step on your journey.

Stay in the passionate flow. When you are in the flow, fully engaged in an activity with intense focus and joy, you are living in harmony with the universe and your place in it. It becomes obvious when one has fallen out of the flow; there is resistance, boredom, apathy, and anxiety. Stay on the path of your bliss.

Do the very best that you can in everything that you choose to do.

Acquire mental poise

As a guide to acquiring mental poise, I paraphrase the words of Miguel Ruiz from his book *"The Four Agreements: A Practical Guide to Personal Freedom"*.

Words are important, be careful of the words you use, speak them with integrity.

Remember that what someone says against you is really about them and people's words can only hurt you if you believe what it is they are saying.

> *"When another person makes you suffer, it is because he suffers deeply within himself, and his suffering is spilling over. He does not need punishment; he needs help. That's the message he is sending."*
>
> ### *Thích Nhất Hạnh*

Do all that you say you'll do, always speak the truth, don't speak or think negatively about yourself, be impeccable in thought, word and actions.

Never assume anything, always have the courage to ask questions.

Don't be a victim of your own life.

Take charge of your life, don't allow circumstances to push and pull you this way and that.

The great Egyptian Alchemist Thoth taught the principles of polarity and rhythm; he showed that things which are considered complete polar opposites are really just two sides of the same thing and that all aspects of life oscillate between such polar opposites in a predictable rhythm.

Even one's moods and emotional states conform to such polar cycles; love to fear, happiness to sadness. When, for example, you find yourself on the downward slide toward sadness, you simply focus upon the opposite pole, happiness, which can be accomplished in this case, by simply smiling.

By altering your focus, you will not experience the descent into undesirable emotional states, and in so doing you will no longer become a victim of your emotions and blind circumstance, but instead master them.

Love and respect your body

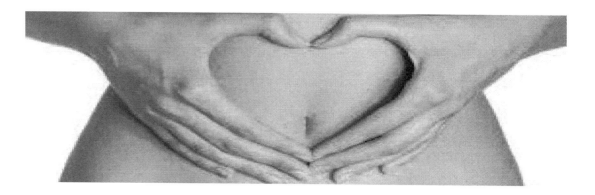

Listen to your body, it is constantly speaking to you, but its voice is quiet.

Eat the least amount of food possible, of a raw, vegan diet based primarily on fresh organic juicy fruits, but fast regularly to liberate the energy needed to repair and maintain the body.

Breathe clean air and drink clean water. Spend lots of time in nature, around trees and plants, and learn to breathe deeply.

Do some kind of physical activity every day.

Get 8 hours (or as many as your body needs) of restful sleep in a darkened and quiet room with plenty of ventilation.

Get plenty of Sunshine.

Physiology Heal Thyself

As previously explained, this universe is not one of physical objects, but a construct of the mind-stuff of an infinite consciousness and as such, most, if not all of our preconceptions of the world must change. One of the biggest misconceptions we have about ourselves is that the human body is a mere clockwork mechanism, a biological machine comprised of discrete parts that wear out or break and can be "fixed" by removing and/or replacing the faulty part.

The body is not a collection of parts, it is an infinitely intelligent whole, a community of trillions of conscious beings bound together through love. Now, I don't mean that pairs of cells are kissing and making out behind the lymph nodes (although from their perspective that might be exactly what is happening) No, not the Hollywood version of love, but the idea of cells doing for their neighbours as they would have done for themselves.

Sound familiar?

There is only one thing that can heal the human body and it's not a drug, nor is it a herb or mysterious energies from a laying on of hands, the only thing that can ever heal the human body is the human body itself. External intervention may stimulate the healing process, or provide much needed energy, but at the end of the day it's the body itself that does the job.

Consider a city composed of several million individuals, such a city's response to a hither-to unknown threat to its health and wellbeing would not a blind mechanistic one but an intelligent one based on an infinite knowledge of its own resources and capabilities. Imagine that the city's water supply had become contaminated with a deadly poison, many thousands might die as a result. One can imagine the workers in the water department might soon determine the cause to be a naturally occurring seam of arsenic progressively seeping into the reservoir that feeds the city.

In an ideal world, the inhabitants might get together and send a huge contingent of people to help remove the arsenic from the water, but this is the modern world and the business of this city is imports and exports, an economy that employs 80% of the inhabitants in processing the constant stream of imported goods, so all personnel who can be spared, from the remaining 20%, are sent and the city suffers from the crippling effects of not only the poison but of the lack of available personnel to keep the city's vital functions operating. In a human, we call these conditions *"symptoms"*.

We can extend the analogy to include the medicinal effects of certain foods if we imagine that certain imports require to be reconstituted with water before being sent out as an export, and using contaminated water is not an option. In that case, the city is then *"stimulated"* into providing more workers to quickly clean up the water to an acceptable level so that commerce can resume.

The effect of pharmaceutical drugs in this example would be like introducing a substantial fire over several blocks in another part of the city, most of those working on water cleanup operations would be drafted in to deal with this, more pressing, matter. The damage caused by the poisoning is still occurring but the city's response to the arsenic poisoning (the symptoms) will decline in favour of the more immediate threat.

From the prevailing allopathic point of view it might appear as if the introduction of the fire has *"treated"* the symptoms of poisoning, but it only appears that way because the city personnel are no longer responding to it, the poison is continuing to cause damage, but now the city also has to deal with the effects of the fire.

When the issue is a long term chronic problem, such as discovering that it is impossible to stop the arsenic from contaminating the reservoir, one can imagine an emergency management group coming up with a plan to divert and hold the incoming water in a disused quarry and feed it to one of the city's two sewerage processing plants, modified and repurposed to filter the arsenic from the water before general distribution. As the plant comes online and becomes more effective at its new role, deaths turn to severe illnesses, then to mild but chronic discomfort.

The general health of the entire city declines a small amount from the low level poisoning and the decline in waste elimination function resulting from running on one sewerage plant instead of two, but the city has successfully adapted to the environmental crisis, but at the cost of its inhabitants' general health and longevity.

The human body adapts to damage, environmental changes or new destructive habits in the same way, pressing so-called redundant organs into service or adapting and repurposing existing organs into new or expanded roles.

* * * *

As an intelligent system, the human body is aware of itself and its own design; Dr. Rupert Sheldrake has extensively researched a branch of biology known as "Morphogenetic Fields" which is the concept that organisms are shaped by fields that serve as an energetic template to which developing organisms conform.

In his book "*Morphic Resonance: The Nature of Formative Causation*" Sheldrake shows how these Morphic fields are self-organizing regions of influence, like magnetic fields that underlie the organisation of proteins, cells, crystals, plants, animals like invisible blueprints that hold the original design of the human body in its perfect form.

This idea provides a glimpse into the mechanics of healing as it implies that there is an energetic or astral body underlying the physical one, so that even if a part of the physical body no longer exists, the template remains to guide its re-growth.

This energetic template was actually measured and reported by Harold S. Burr, a neuroanatomist, in a series of articles entitled *"Electrical Characteristics of Living Systems"* and *"The Electro-Dynamic Theory of Life"* in 1935. Burr found that young salamanders were surrounded by an electrical field shaped like an adult salamander and the same field was even present around the unfertilised egg.

This is an intriguing idea since it explains the phenomenon of phantom limb syndrome, where an amputee still feels sensations in the missing limb, and suggests that the human body is capable of re-growing severed limbs if its processes are not interfered with because the energetic template still exists even if the physical limb does not.

The conventional medical approach to severed digits or limbs is to pump the patient full of antibiotics and tetanus vaccines that inhibit the body's ability to repair (as it now has to deal with more acutely poisonous substances) and then sew up and cauterise the wound, preventing the body from performing any of its natural regeneration procedures.

However, in 2010 a company called **ACell** introduced a new product, a powder comprised of stem cells from a pig's bladder, which was able to re-grow not only fingers but thigh muscle and many other tissues.

It should be noted that human urine is an excellent source of human stem cells and are likely to work far more efficiently than those from a pig's urinary tract.

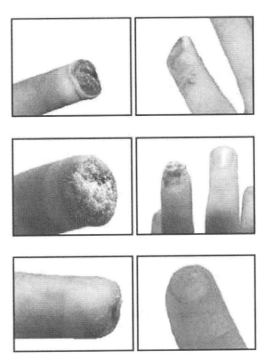

ACell's MatriStem powder used to re-grow fingers.

The Body-Mind Connection

Since this universe is a mental construct, everything in it can be considered as a metaphor.

As ridiculous as it might sound, the feelings that you experience when dealing with someone who is annoying, frustrating and pedantic, might literally manifest as a pain in the neck

You can think of yourself as having three bodies. As well as the physical body, you have an emotional body and a mental one. All three are linked so that a change in one affects the others. A thought in your mental body, such as *"Who the hell does he think he is!"* might cause a feeling of anger to appear in the emotional body which in turn produces a manifestation of symptoms in the physical.

When the non-physical, spiritual part of you has a thought in the mental body, a chemical cascade, corresponding to the emotion evoked by the thought, occurs within the body. It is a unique chemical cocktail which is experienced as a feeling and prepares the body for the consequences of the emotion.

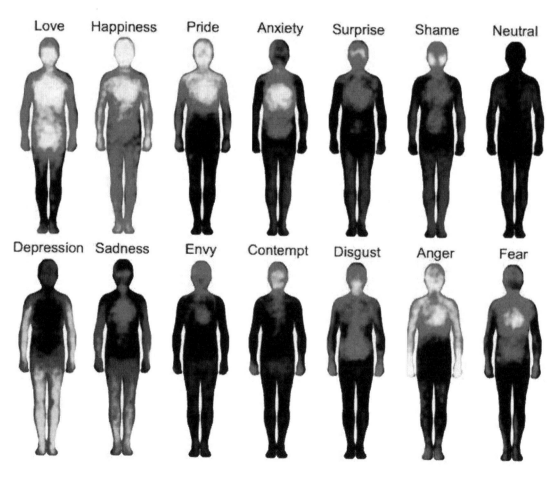

How emotions are mapped upon the human body.

94

If the emotion is, for example, fear, then the chemical signals the release of stress hormones that cause the heart to beat faster and the blood to move out to the extremities in preparation for the sudden explosion of muscle utilisation. The immune system and higher brain functions are shut down and a host of other changes take place to conserve energy and enhance the instinctive survival responses so the body is ready to run or fight at a moment's notice.

The biologist, Dr. Bruce Lipton in his book, *"The Biology of Belief,"* notes that there are just two emotions at opposite ends of an emotional scale, Love and Fear, and that all other emotions are just different degrees along that scale. This corresponds with the two opposite states that the human body exists in, and that is either Growth or Protection.

So if the emotional body is in the state of Love then the physical body is in the state of Growth, and its energy is directed toward renewing billions of cells, repairing injuries and maintaining systems, keeping you alive and healthy. But if the emotional body is in the state of Fear then the physical body redirects the energy away from cell renewal and repair operations and prepares itself to run or fight. Indeed, the switch from Growth to Protection can be so abrupt and so violent that the growth measures shut down too quickly and the body can literally be frightened to death.

Unfortunately, the fear response is only meant as an emergency measure, and under chronic or prolonged stress the effects of cell degradation, because energy is not available to replace them, coupled with protracted exposure to the stress hormones can cause significant and long term damage to various organs.

In the short term, these measures suppress the "immune system" which regulates the actions of bacteria and viruses that naturally inhabit the physical body. These so-called opportunistic viruses can now multiply unchecked and take hold.

One of the hallmarks of our modern culture is that the mass media keeps us in a state of perpetual stress and fear.

So, there is a psychological trigger for what allopathic medicine calls illness or disease. Diseases are not the result of the external activities of dangerous germs, bacteria, viruses, carcinogens and the like. Rather, they stem from a thought pattern that results in a particular cocktail of hormones and stress chemicals or endorphins which we experience as an emotion.

This chemical concoction is designed to prepare the body for the consequences of the particular thought pattern until the situation is dealt with, but chronic, deep seated emotion held for prolonged periods will weaken and even damage particular organs and tissues, and trigger healing symptoms.

As a quick rule of thumb:

Anger: Releases chemicals that weaken the Liver

Grief: Releases chemicals that weaken the Lungs

Worry: Releases chemicals that weaken the Stomach

Stress: Releases chemicals that weaken the Heart and Brain

Fear: Releases chemicals that weaken the Kidneys

That is why some people can smoke 100 cigarettes a day and never get lung cancer and yet another who would be considered a light smoker but suffering long term effects of grief will succumb. One of the things missing from the allopathic cause and effect model is the mental / emotional aspect.

The allopathic approach to illness, which is to ignore the physical and psychological causes of the illness and mask the symptoms, virtually ensures that the underlying issue will manifest at some later date in a far more serious manner as it is allowed to progress unchallenged and the patient is rendered unaware that the issue still exists.

Treating the issue by neutralising the underlying physical and emotional (chemical) imbalances will remedy the problem, but unless the thought or behavioural patterns in the mental body are addressed then the patterns will continue to cycle around and the problem will return.

Allowing the body to heal the immediate injury is only part of the story. In order to prevent a recurrence, the thought pattern and emotional response must be addressed.

What's a Meta For?

Our consciousness operates the human body and, through it, our universe using metaphor and symbolism.

In a universe of conscious mind-stuff, metaphors are immensely powerful: the placebo effect is a direct expression of that power.

The placebo effect works because the sugar pill represents healing in the mind of the patient and the more powerful the representation, the more effective the healing. And so fake injections are more effective than a sugar pill and likewise a fake surgery is even more effective than a bogus injection simply because of the distinction in the patients mind that surgery is more efficacious that an injection and that translates into a greater level of healing that the patient's body performs as a response.

A metaphor is a mental construct that your consciousness uses to operate the human body and the universe beyond it. That is why Cannabis is such an effective *"medicine"*, not because of its chemical effects on the physical body but because of its effects on the mind and its belief systems.

The hands and the interplay of bones, muscles, gravity and leverage, are a metaphor for moving and manipulating the energy fields that we perceive as things that we believe we have no direct control over. Telekinesis, the ability to move objects with the mind, is another such metaphor that is just as valid as the hands to achieve the same thing. However, while this ability has been verified by many anecdotal sources, the medical and scientific establishment have been successful in discrediting such abilities as mere fantasy, so in the minds of the public, the metaphor loses its validity and so, no habit is formed that brings telekinesis into regular use.

Because the metaphor of moving things with our hands is so much easier to comprehend and perform than that of moving objects with the power of our minds, that then becomes the prevailing habit, and relegates Telekinesis to the backwaters of Parapsychology.

But why is habit so important?

Habits: We become what we repeatedly do

The Hermetic principle of vibration states that:

> *"All is in motion... Nothing rests"*

This is true for everything in what we have learned to call reality, even the immutable *"Laws of Nature"*.

The universal constants that govern gravitation, the speed of light, the charge of an electron are not fixed and unchanging. The so-called fixed, immutable laws of nature are more akin to habits, that is, once some new process or state is achieved in one part of the system then it becomes successively easier for that process or state to reoccur anywhere else in the system until at some point it becomes the default state and some human in a white lab coat will come along and declare it is a universal law.

Imagine that between two towns there is a thick, impenetrable forest and travellers are forced to trek many miles around it, taking many hours to go between the two. Eventually one traveller, fed up with the journey, decides to hack his way through the forest. It is very difficult and he fails to get very far on his first attempt but his persistence pays off and he finally makes it through to the other side of the forest. The next traveller to pass that way might notice that there is a slightly less dense way through the trees and he is tempted to push through and is rewarded with a much shorter trip. As more travellers follow suit, a path begins to form, the path becomes a track, then widens to a road and eventually becomes the M25 (and so goes back to taking many hours to get anywhere).

Before Roger Bannister, the idea that a human could run a mile in under 4 minutes was impossible, now the record is broken at least every 4 years at the Olympics.

This is the essence of *"Morphic Resonance"* and Dr. Rupert Sheldrake has performed many experiments proving this theory. It is well known that rats take a fairly consistent length of time to learn a new maze. Sheldrake constructed a new maze in London and allowed a group of rats to learn it, then in Sydney, Australia another group of rats were exposed to the same maze for the first time and they solved it significantly quicker than the original rats as well as much quicker than a control group that were exposed to a similarly complex but untried maze.

Sheldrake also recounts the story that his teenage son and friends used morphic resonance to their advantage during school exams. As public school examinations use the exact same papers, and all participants sit the exam at the exact same time across the country, young Sheldrake reasoned that if they were to start with the last five questions first before going back to question one then they could take advantage of morphic resonance since by that time, thousands of students would have already answered these questions. Sure enough, young Sheldrake and his pals received much higher than average test scores.

Another important factor is that it has been shown, through experimentation, that the placebo effect is even more successful if the doctor administering it is convinced of the placebo's efficacy. This suggests that a substance could be imbued with healing properties by people who believe that it has them; similarly a harmless, inert substance could be mistakenly imbued with the intention that it is poisonous by the misguided belief and conviction of a chemist in Bombay, India and subsequently a man in Dundee, Scotland might fall sick after ingesting it. And as the idea that the substance is poison gains ground, more people experience sickness after contact with it, warnings are issued to the public, labels with the skull and crossbones appear on bottles and so a habit is formed and is considered self evident.

This is why Yogic Masters are able to ingest and transmute deadly poisons, because they are not transmuting a physical substance, they are transmuting the **idea** that the substance is poisonous.

It follows that no matter what issue we may face, we can find a set of metaphors that would enable us to instruct the body to heal itself.

First of all, we must remember that symptoms are not the terrifying demons that we have been told they are, they are warning signs that the body is dealing with an issue, typically by elimination of toxins. There is nothing we really need do except getting out of the body's way, but unfortunately the metaphors we employ in our modern lifestyle do not ordinarily allow us that luxury: we eat to *"keep our strength up"*; we take the medical profession's pills and potions to mask the symptoms with acute poisoning; and, once we can no longer experience the warning messages, we continue with our normal routines oblivious to the energy deficiency, caused by our actions, actively preventing our bodies from healing.

Listening to your body

Your body is an intelligent metropolis of conscious beings. Each and every one of them is as much you as all of them combined. But because of our upbringing, our education and our ongoing media programming, we believe that we live in our heads, and only on the left hand side.

The accommodation in the left hemisphere of the brain has become very comfortable and we are so used to associating ourselves with the function served by this lobe that we have settled in and developed a self aware survival and protection mechanism called the Ego.

A mosaic of St. Ambrose.

The manifestation of the ego would seem to be a relatively recent development. In the early 4th Century, St. Augustine of Hippo in his Confessions (Book VI) speaks about visiting St. Ambrose of Milan. Augustine walked into the room where Ambrose was sitting and was shocked to see that he was reading a book without speaking aloud.

This was a feat unheard of in those days and would suggest that the people of that era possessed no inner monologue, no constant internal chatter, pretending to be us. Indeed, the fact that it was this period in history when ordinary people would occasionally hear a voice in their heads and attribute it to God or demons would suggest that this was the first beginning of the ego.

The ego's primary role is protection and survival, and it has been relentlessly programmed by media, culture and societal norms using liberal doses of fear and exploiting the desire for the safety of conformity.

The problem is that we have begun to believe that the ego is actually who we are.

Your body provides you with a constant stream of information and advice but these quiet *"voices"* are overshadowed by our head dominated mentality and the constant chatter of our ego. We tend to ignore or misread our body's messages, for example, your bodily functions become depressed, your energy levels are low, your concentration is impaired. Your body is telling you that it requires rest, but your mind might say,

"I just have to finish this report"

So you continue working, or worse still, you might ingest some artificial stimulant like Coffee or a so-called *"Energy Drink"* to irritate the body into action.

A common scenario where we ignore the body's messages.

Sometimes, completely contrary to what our bodies are telling us and indeed logic, we even go for a run or do a workout because we think we need to *"energise"* ourselves while we rob the body of its last reserves of energy. Rest actually means doing absolutely nothing, no paperwork, no Facebook, no cell phone calls, nothing.

The best example of how we misinterpret messages from the body would be the feeling of hunger. If you were to ask one hundred people how they experience hunger it is likely that you would get a hundred different answers.

Most people have not allowed themselves to stop eating long enough to experience true hunger, most are so well fed that they can no longer tell the difference between hunger and a vague feeling of discomfort in the lower abdomen or a feeling of anxiety, tiredness, boredom, stress or any number of psychological, emotional or physical stimuli.

We also misinterpret various sensations that emanate from the stomach area as evidence of hunger. Some of these sensations, such as rumbling, can be attributed to an anticipation of a habitual feeding routine. Cravings for food can also be brought on by a Pavlovian response to seeing or smelling food, a trick that has not been missed by advertisers and purveyors of processed non-foods as they fill the air around their establishments with the enticing smells of their wares.

But the greatest cause of non-specific, generalised food cravings is in fact an irritation of the stomach lining. The foods we eat actually irritate the stomach lining and as the stomach becomes empty the already irritated stomach walls come into contact with one another and cause the gnawing feelings of discomfort that is mistaken as hunger. Most people do not intuitively know exactly where the spleen is in their body, or their liver, pancreas, gall bladder or any number of other organs. In fact, as a rule, we only become aware of the internal location of our organs when they become irritated, inflamed or dysfunctional in some way: we only feel our kidneys when they become over worked; we feel our stomach when we eat and irritate the stomach lining, and we feel it again when it's emptiness further aggravates the problem.

The difficulty arises from our left hemisphere communication bias. Although we are aware that most of our communication is non-verbal, our conscious mind is dominated by language. We speak using words, we think in words and we subsequently expect that all communication of any importance will come in this form. However, the true language of the body is feeling, emotions and internal pictures, that is, internal representations of a concept, or in other words, metaphors and symbolism.

I had direct experience of this communication one morning in 2011.

I was awoken at about 2am with a nose bleed. I used to get nosebleeds quite regularly as a child and so I had developed various strategies to deal with them, however, this one would not stop.

By 3am I had tried everything I could think of to stop the flow to no avail. I was tired and had to get up for work in another four hours so I stuffed my nose with cotton wool and tried to get some sleep knowing full well that the blood would simply pool in my sinus cavity, but as my head hit the pillow I began to feel a burning sensation on the back of my neck.

As I lay there looking for the cool side of the pillow, my neck got hotter and hotter to the point where I simply had to get up. But, instead of doing the obvious, that is, listening to the message and responding appropriately, as child of the technological age, I went straight to the internet and searched for *"nosebleed burning sensation back of neck"* but nothing relevant seemed to be returned. I was just about to give up when I clicked on a link that caught my eye and right there in the middle of the page it said:

"To stop a nosebleed, place a cold flannel on the back of the neck"

I tried it and not only did the nosebleed stop, but the burning sensation also disappeared immediately.

My body had sent me a clear, unequivocal message:

> *"Put something cold here!"*

But it didn't come in a form that I considered important, so I ignored its rather obvious meaning and searched for a logical left-brained interpretation instead.

Responding to your body's messages

As previously noted, the human body is a conscious, intelligent, self repairing organisation and that when it provides a warning, in the form of a symptom, it actually means that the body is already dealing with the problem and providing you information on how to assist its repair efforts.

So, contrary to what we have been taught, symptoms are not evil or a problem to be dealt with, they are actually a good thing, a sign that the body is already on the case. It is telling you:

> *"Hey relax, I got this, here's what I need you to do..."*

Unfortunately, the approach that the white coated allopathic priests – or doctors as they like to call themselves – advocate is to prescribe one type of toxin that deadens the nerves or another type of poison that provides the body with a more acute problem to deal with so that its resources are switched away from the original problem, effectively masking the body's messages and fooling the patient into believing that the issue is resolved. Consequently the patient resumes normal life, unable to receive the body's instructions, eating and energy expenditure resumes, and so the body no longer has the available energy to deal with the poisonous effects of the pharmaceuticals or the original problem which eventually is allowed to become a chronic one.

The message is usually so obvious that we miss its importance, but in general the correct response is usually the immediate, intuitive one, before our logical mind kicks in and overlays the body's intelligence with society's programmed *"wisdom"*.

Here are a few examples:

> *"I feel sick; I don't feel like eating... But I'd better eat something to keep my strength up."*

"I have a headache; I need to lie down... But I have to get back to work; I'd better take a Paracetamol."

"I have a fever; I need to sleep... But I'd better take something to bring my temperature down."

It is likely that you recognise at least one of the above scenarios from your own life, where you have overlaid your intuitive reaction to a symptom with a logical thought pattern that runs in direct opposition to what your body needs you to do and so hinders its ability to heal.

The process of coughing, for example, has been labelled as a symptom of disease by the allopathic fraudsters, but in fact is a natural but emergency measure employed by the body to forcefully expel pollution, poisonous gases and acids from the lungs. Our natural intuitive response to coughing would be to remove ourselves from the poisonous environment. But, instead, we take a poisonous allopathic remedy to suppress the cough so that we can continue to comfortably breathe the poisonous air that our lungs were attempting to purge themselves of.

The correct response to all such symptoms is usually the first intuitive "feeling" that you don't have to think about, but this is often quickly followed by a thought process that directly contravenes the intent of your feelings.

So to summarise, we need to change our relationship to our symptoms; they are not the terrifying demons that we have been told they are. They are warning signs that the body is dealing with an issue, typically by elimination of toxins.

There is nothing we really need do except get out of the body's way, but unfortunately the metaphors we employ in our modern lifestyle do not ordinarily allow us that luxury: we eat to *"keep our strength up"*; we take the medical profession's pills and potions to mask the symptoms with acute poisoning; and, once we can no longer experience the warning messages, we continue with our normal routines oblivious to the harm and energy deficiency, caused by our actions, actively preventing our bodies from healing.

Reprogramming the body

When you are not mindful of the present moment then your body will default to subconscious programming, in exactly the same way if you are not mindful during a drive to work, then your subconscious Drive-To-Work program will operate the car and negotiate the streets while your mind is elsewhere. Most of our daily life is conducted in this way and so we find ourselves with very little control over our bodies, or indeed our lives.

I have explained that thought patterns, which are established as subconscious programs from childhood, cause a chemical cascade of hormones and biochemicals, which are experienced as emotions and eventually manifest in the physical body as symptoms. The way to reprogram the body away from these automatic programs is to disassociate from the thought pattern so that the emotional response is not automatic.

Many times throughout the day, we hear our own internal voice as constant brain chatter, commenting on the things that we are experiencing, replaying the past and projecting into the future.

Which voice do you listen to?

If you were to take some time to listen carefully to what that voice is saying, something very odd will eventually occur to you.

"If I am listening to what this voice is saying, then who is speaking?"

I had this experience in 2013 while I was working at an eco-village. I found myself working alone in a kitchen that a group of us were supposed to be building; I looked out of the window and saw a few of the others sitting around on the grass relaxing and I could hear my inner voice growling angrily,

"Why am I the only bastard working? What the hell are those guys over there doing lounging about while I am working my arse off??"

At this point I remember thinking:

"Wow, he sounds angry"

But I noted that I didn't actually feel angry myself and it suddenly dawned on me that *"I"* was making that observation, so who was the angry voice?

I settled back and listened to the voice rant and rage as I continued to work but from my new perspective as the observer of this thinker. I was no longer attached to this voice and so there were no emotional consequence to its words, and therefore there were no symptoms within the physical body or ensuing dramas in the physical universe.

This *"thinker"* is your ego. It is not you!

The ego is a powerful subconscious program designed to protect you and usually repeatedly focuses upon negative aspects of your life. However, once you become aware of it and become practiced at detaching from it, you can reprogram it by overwriting the thought pattern with a new pattern that better serves your mental and physical wellbeing.

If, for example, you find yourself thinking thoughts like:

"You can't do this, you aren't good enough, every time you've tried you've failed and if you try again then everyone will know you are a failure"

Should you decide to attach to this pattern you would most likely start experiencing anxiety, worry and fear, there may be a sinking feeling in the stomach, profuse sweating and your hands might start shaking. If these emotions are repeated over and over again then symptoms would begin to appear as a response to the continued exposure to the chemical signature of these stress hormones.

From your place of detachment, however, you can see that your ego is referring to past experiences that reinforce this idea and is protecting you from future humiliation by preventing you from taking action and pre-programming you to fail should you make an attempt.

You can rewrite this thought pattern as soon as you recognise it by repeating to yourself:

"I can do this, I am more than good enough, I learn more every time, I do better every time"

Rather than just say the words, you need to feel them. Feel how it feels to be more than capable, see yourself performing the action with grace and ease and imagine how you feel after a job well done. It takes practice but you will find that it was the ego's focus on the negative outcome that was drawing that outcome toward you and by overlaying the ego with an alternative focus you will draw a different outcome into reality.

This life is a game, a game that you chose to play and at every moment of every day your life is playing out exactly as you wish it to, even if it seems pretty shitty right now. The trouble is that if you don't realise that you are playing a game then the game plays you and you will find yourself being swung around by circumstance from one crisis to the next in a life and a world that makes no sense whatsoever. However, once you become aware that you are playing and you find a rulebook and instruction manual then you find that you are in a magical playground able to experience anything could possibly imagine.

You are an infinite, immortal being, playing in a physical three dimensional realm using a biological Earth Rover, which is recording every detail of your game play for later review. You cannot do anything wrong (although, it appears that unlearned lessons will be repeated with increasing levels of discomfort and intensity).

*   *   *   *

Even if you cannot possibly imagine that the universe works in the way described in this book, then I invite you re-read this book to this point while pretending that it does.

If you hold this belief within your heart and act upon it accordingly you will find it works just the same.

In other words:

> *"Fake it until you make it".*

Emergency Repairs

In day to day life, accidents, mishaps and circumstances occur that cause problems and minor symptoms. While the severity of each of problems can be wide ranging, in most cases they are not serious and most people pick something up at the chemist or get some pharmaceutical poison from an important looking chap in a white coat.

Unfortunately, if the cause of the symptoms is not addressed or the body is not allowed to repair itself then the problem will escalate.

What follows is a selection of remedies for some of life's little mishaps:

Headaches

Most recurring headaches are due to tension or are a symptom of poisoning.

The particular type of stress that causes headaches ultimately stems from fear and or self criticism. Taking time out to meditate regularly and addressing the fear based, or self critical, thought patterns will prevent the triggering of this type of headache.

There are also two types of poisoning that may be involved in causing headaches. Sugary foods or those containing artificial sweeteners such as Aspartame are usually responsible in this case, so cut out sweets, chocolate bars, cakes and fizzy drinks etc. Or, if the headaches are accompanied with coughing, sneezing or lethargy, then it is likely that the air is being progressively toxified due to inadequate ventilation. Opening windows and being mindful of the air quality will prevent reoccurrence of headaches.

Urine Therapy is very effective in treating headaches. If one were to drink their own urine twice a day then the attacks would tend to subside within a week to ten days. In milder cases, simply massaging fresh cool urine into the neck, forehead, temples and behind the ears may be sufficient.

Ear pain or infection

Because the ear, nose and throat are connected, ear problems can be tackled by using drops of fresh urine in the ears, nose or by gargling urine. Place several drops of fresh urine in the ears and plug the ears with cotton balls soaked in olive oil to prevent leakage. Sometimes people experience more severe ear pain after using urine – this is known as a detoxification symptom or a healing crisis.

Urine stimulates the body to eliminate toxins and those toxins need to find a route out of the body, which tend to be the point of weakness in the body. So, should ear pain ensue, the best course of action is to continue the treatment until all the toxins have been eliminated.

This might sound counterproductive. You're trying to get rid of the symptoms right? Why would you use something that will make things worse?

We have been conditioned to believe that symptoms are an evil that must be eliminated as quickly as possible. This is a false perspective. Symptoms are a sign that the body is healing or eliminating toxins and rather than masking these symptoms with pharmaceuticals, the use of urine in this way aids the body in the process of eliminating and healing.

Mouth ulcers, Toothache

For mouth ulcers, gum inflammation, toothaches and abscesses, collect the first midstream urination of the day and rinse the mouth with about two to four tablespoons of urine, swishing it around the mouth, and pulling through the teeth for about twenty minutes.

Within ten to fifteen minutes even the most excruciating tooth pain will disappear, gum inflammation will subside and ulcers will begin to heal. If this process is repeated a few times a day over the course of a week, then abscesses, infections and decayed teeth will start to become healthy.

Cuts, bruises and burns

Soak gauze or cotton wool with urine (aged urine is usually more effective but fresh is almost as good if aged urine is not available). Place the gauze on the site of the cut or burn and hold it in place by wrapping it with cling film. Keep the area moist with additional applications of urine and by changing the dressing regularly.

Urine, applied to a wound or burn, will almost immediately staunch bleeding and stop pain, and because of its antiseptic and disinfectant properties it will prevent the occurrence of infections and gangrene. The area should be healed within three days with little or no scarring. Urine is so effective at healing wounds and burns that John Armstrong in his book "The Water of Life" describes urine as:

"...flesh, blood and vital tissues in living solution"

Bites, stings and itchiness

Bites, stings, itchiness or any skin irritations can be treated with fresh urine massaged into the site of the bite or sting. Any pain should be relieved in seconds, redness and inflammation will disappear within minutes.

Collect urine ten to fifteen seconds after the bite or sting occurs and gently massage into the affected area, repeating every hour until all signs of injury have gone.

For significant bites, such as from an animal, immediately wash the wound thoroughly with urine collected ten to fifteen seconds after the incident. Then place a urine soaked gauze or cotton wool pad (Urine Pack) over the wound and keep moist with periodic applications of either fresh or aged urine.

If the bite is from a poisonous snake or spider, it should also be washed and treated in the same manner, but additionally drink the remainder of the urine apart from approximately ten drops which are placed under the tongue and held there for at least 20 minutes.

Repeat this process until all signs of adverse reactions have ceased.

Sore Throat

For sore throats, tonsillitis and hoarseness, collect the first midstream urination of the day and use three to four tablespoons to gargle with and then rinse the mouth with about two to four tablespoons of urine, swishing it around the mouth, and pulling through the teeth for about twenty minutes.

Allergic reactions

When an allergic reaction occurs, wait ten to fifteen seconds after the first symptoms appear, collect some urine and put ten drops under the tongue and hold them there for as long as possible, swallow and repeat until the symptoms subside. If this process is repeated every time the symptoms reoccur then sensitivity to the allergen will also begin to subside.

Another approach to the long term treatment of allergies is to collect some urine at the height of the allergy symptoms and make a homeopathic urine preparation as described in **Appendix I** and treat reoccurrences with several drops of the homeopathic preparation every two to three hours until the symptoms fade.

Poisoning

In cases of poisoning (food poisoning or otherwise), wait ten to fifteen seconds then collect some urine and drink as much as can be tolerated. Your urine will contain homeopathic amounts of antigens to the poison or food contaminant, that is, information that stimulates the body to produce antibodies and to eliminate toxins.

Place ten drops of urine under the tongue and hold there for at least 20 minutes, this will also reduce the symptoms associated with the poison. Repeat this process hourly until symptoms subside. If possible, go for a run or engage in some exercise that would promote deep and rapid breathing as the primary method of elimination of ingested toxins is through the lungs.

For the following 3 to 5 days eat no food, fast on pure water (preferably distilled) and urine.

Acne, Eczema and Psoriasis

When eczema appears, use aged urine – that is, collect urine in a dark glass bottle, stop the bottle with a wad of cotton wool to allow the urine to breath and store in a cool dark place.

Pour a little into the palm of the hand and massage into the affected area until it completely absorbs into the skin and becomes completely dry. The urine does not leave a smell on the skin once absorbed (even very smelly old urine).

When it is a baby that has eczema, wash the affected area with the baby's own wet nappy then gently massage in until completely absorbed.

Sore, Blistered or Chapped Hands

Place urine, preferably aged urine, in a bowl and wash the hands thoroughly for several minutes, then rub the hands together until the hands are dry.

If the hands are badly blistered then use a **Urine Pack** (soak a gauze or cotton wool pad with urine) and place over the sores or blisters and hold it in place by wrapping it with cling film, keep the area moist with additional applications of urine. Alternatively, place a little urine inside a latex glove and loosely seal the hands within using tape or elastic bands so that the affected skin is in constant contact with the urine as long as possible. The skin on the hands should be completely healed within a few days.

Splinters

For a deep, inaccessible splinter one would use a similar process to cuts and burns.

Make up a **Urine Pack** by soaking a gauze or cotton wool pad with urine, place over the splinter and hold it in place by wrapping it with cling film, keep the area moist with additional applications of urine.

The urine stimulates the body to eliminate toxins or anything that does not belong there, so after three days the splinter will be found in the dressing not in the body.

Infections

Infections, both internal and external, can be treated with the body's own urine. Make up a **Urine Pack** by soaking a gauze or cotton wool pad with urine and place over the site of the infection and hold it in place by wrapping it with cling film, keep the area moist with additional applications of urine.

The internal indications of infection such fever, chills, nausea, diarrhoea and vomiting are best addressed by performing basic urine therapy, that is, collect and drink the first midstream urination of the morning, saving a little to massage into the body (see Appendix I)

If this process is repeated late afternoon/early evening then all signs of infection should abate within a few days.

Broken bones

Dealing with broken bones and trauma care are the only issues that the allopathic medical establishment is effective at treating because that treatment essentially consists of immobilising the limb and allowing the body to heal itself.

Place a **Urine Pack** on the break by soaking a gauze or cotton wool pad with urine and place over the site of the infection and hold it in place by wrapping it with cling film, or a bandage, then immobilise the limb with a splint made up of any suitable materials available, such as tree branches, metal pipe etc. Keep the area continually moist with additional applications of urine.

Basic urine therapy should be started immediately, that is, collect and drink the first midstream urination of the morning, saving a little to massage into the body (see Appendix I) and repeated late afternoon/early evening.

The body should undergo complete rest and no food should be taken for at least three days after which occasional small light meals of mostly juicy fruit or leafy green salads may be taken between two to three day fasts.

Broken limbs treated in this fashion should be healed within two to three weeks.

Rejuvenation from "old age"

While old age may not seem like a situation that can be repaired, the truth is that the human body is not affected, in any way, by the number of times the Earth orbits the Sun. What we refer to as "old age" is merely the body's lifelong accumulation of toxins coupled with subconscious programming and toxic thought patterns. As soon as the toxins are eliminated and the toxic thought patterns are reprogrammed the signs of "old age" begin to disappear.

Avoiding the intake of toxins in the modern world is nearly impossible, but it is possible to reduce the toxic load to levels that the body can more easily manage. This can be accomplished by changing the diet away from meat, dairy, sugar, salt, processed, genetically altered and cooked foods and toward raw juicy fruits, nuts and light leafy green vegetables. The size and frequency of such meals should also be reduced and interspersed with regular two to three day fasts.

The body, while ordinarily efficient at eliminating toxins, can be greatly assisted by urine therapy and distilled water. Drinking urine twice a day, with at least one urine massage will help to stimulate the body to eliminate toxins. However, the more urine you consume and massage into the skin, the better the results.

Also, drinking distilled water to a combined total of a gallon (four litres) per day will dissolve and wash accumulated inorganic minerals out of the body.

Fasting is also important for this process as it liberates the energy necessary for the body to eliminate and repair the tissues and organs. Once the body has become accustomed to two to three day fasts then progress to week long fasts where only distilled water and urine are consumed.

The final part of this process involves reprogramming the thought pattern that expects that the body will wither and grow old and infirm by virtue of the number of candles on a birthday cake. The human body is never more than seven years old as it is constantly rebuilding and renewing itself, the mental picture that people hold that says that an individual of a particular age can no longer do this or that, or is likely to look a certain way is erroneous.

This view can be reframed by visualising oneself in the prime of one's life, remembering in detail how it feels, imagining what that person would be doing right now and how that would feel, and once that picture is fixed in absolute minute detail then **be that person right now**. Act as if you were that person in the prime of their life, and if the voice of the ego is heard to say things like:

> *"I'm too old to be doing this..."*

> *"I'm not getting any younger..."*

> *"I should take it easy, I'm not a young man anymore..."*

Recognise these thought patterns when they occur and overwrite them with details of the visualisation and do not allow these patterns to dictate actions.

> *"I can do this!"*

> *"I am young!"*

> *"This is easy, I'm still young!"*

After three months of following a program such as this, signs of "old age" will reverse and people will begin to remark upon some noticeable changes.

Maintenance

Diet

To reasonably get the best out of your human body, reduce the quantity and density of the food, while increasing the quality of the little that is consumed, interspersed with periods of fasting.

The quality and density of food intake can be improved by totally abandoning the following foodstuffs:

- Sugar.
- Salt.
- Chillies, spices and condiments.
- Cereals and grains such as wheat.
- Bread, cakes, pies, pizza, pastries, pancakes.
- Meat.
- Dairy products.
- Rice, pasta and starchy foods.
- Coffee.
- Carbonated drinks.
- Processed foods.
- Genetically modified food.
- Dense "earthy" vegetables.
- Cooked foods.

These items can be replaced with:

- Fresh organically grown juicy fruits.
- Nuts.
- Seeds.
- Coconut water.
- Coconut oil.
- Fresh organically grown mushrooms.
- Light leafy green vegetables.
- Distilled water.
- Urine.

Food intake should be gradually reduced, if possible, to one small meal per day, with perhaps the occasional snack of berries, nuts or seeds. There should also be periods of fasting from three to seven days at a stretch.

This might seem a daunting prospect but as previously stated in this book, food is an irrelevancy, an addictive substance that once your body begins to purge itself of, appetite will disappear, energy levels will increase and the mood and temperament will lift.

Environment

As previously noted, very little attention is given to the environment within which we exist. We are generally crowded together in dirty, noisy towns and cities, breathing toxic polluted air while bathed in a soup of electro-magnetic radiation.

The houses we live in are poorly ventilated, recto-linear constructions that prevent air and indeed energy from adequately circulating; they shield us from fresh air, sunshine and distilled water, and ultimately cut us off from our connection to the natural world around us.

And more fundamentally, some of us live in regions of the planet that we were not designed to inhabit. The human body has a thin delicate skin, devoid of fur and so not conducive to a cold, wet or icy climate and, as such, the body has had to adapt with its attendant loss of vitality and lifespan.

Unfortunately for most people, changing their environment is not an option, but if possible the ideal would be to move to a more remote area away from cities and towns in a well ventilated dwelling in the midst of nature. Also, spend more time out in nature, in sunshine, and directly connected with the earth and meditating in beautiful countryside. The health benefits of such a change of environment are incalculable.

Mental Attitude

Stress is the most prolific anonymous mass murderer the world has ever known. As we saw while exploring the Body-Mind Connection, all disease stems from a thought pattern and the result is an emergency chemical and hormonal release that we experience as an emotion, which places stress on the body.

There are other sources of stress that only appear in the modern world, such as work worries, financial problems, fear of terrorism, the problem is that the body is not designed to cope with such persistent and chronic stress levels.

In the corporate world stress is considered a good thing. For example, the ability to work under crushing levels of stress is a prized attribute on a successful C.V., but while this ability might get lots of widgets made or TPS reports filed, it provides no benefits to the one under stress. Only illness, premature aging and dependence on stimulants can result – known in the trade as "Burnout".

Here are a few tips to avoid burnout:

- Recognise and remove all sources of stress.
- Turn off the television.
- Reduce your dependence on money.
- Take up a hobby that you enjoy.
- Spend time with friends and family and cultivate healthy relationships with them.
- Adopt a positive mental attitude.
- Set aside time for meditation.
- Get plenty of sunshine, rest and relaxation.

About the Author

In the spring of 2011, I was in deep trouble but I was utterly and blissfully unaware.

I was hugely overweight, nearly 20 stones (127kg), my lungs were those of a 70 year old, because I had suffered with Asthma since childhood and spent decades spraying all sorts of steroids and other pharmaceutical poisons into them, I'd suffered nerve damage in one side of my foot as well as constant pain up the back of my ankle up to my calf muscle from an operation on my Achilles Tendon four years earlier, that made walking long distances difficult.

I had seriously high blood pressure which placed me firmly within stroke territory, and my right shoulder joint would grind bone against bone which made it painful to lift my arm above head height.

I'd also been plagued with a constant ache in my lower back that made standing still for any length of time very tiring indeed and I looked like a very sprightly 55 to 60 year old despite only being 48 at the time.

May 2011, the artist formally known as Pizza the Hutt

It seems inconceivable to me now but even though I was tired, asthmatic and obese, I couldn't run or perform much in the way of physical exercise and was slowly spiralling down into old age and infirmity, I had actually considered myself to be in pretty good health.

My first inkling that this was not a natural state of affairs was a few years earlier when I read a book by G. Edward Griffin called "*A World Without Cancer*" in which he laid bare the whole fraudulent cancer industry. This started me on a journey to find an alternative to the evil medical establishment and their "*Deathcare*" system.

Back to the spring of 2011, I attended the "*Truthjuice Gathering*" in North Wales and listened to a talk on alternative therapies by a lady called Sylvia Chandler who introduced me to the concept of Urine Therapy, now I had vaguely heard about this practice but like most other people I thought of it as something the mentally ill did if left unsupervised or what plane crash victims did to survive once they had eaten the last of the chartered accountants, but I walked out of Sylvia's talk a changed man and I drank my first glass of urine the very next day.

Three years later, I am just under 12 stones (75kg) my lungs have repaired themselves, I no longer have Asthma, the nerve damage and pain in my ankle are gone, my blood pressure is normal, my shoulder and back are like new, the flexibility has returned to my limbs, I can break-dance again and sit in the full lotus position (something I have been unable to do since my 20's) My hair has started to grow back and the lines and wrinkles on my face have disappeared, and my body has literally reverted to as it was when I was in my twenties.

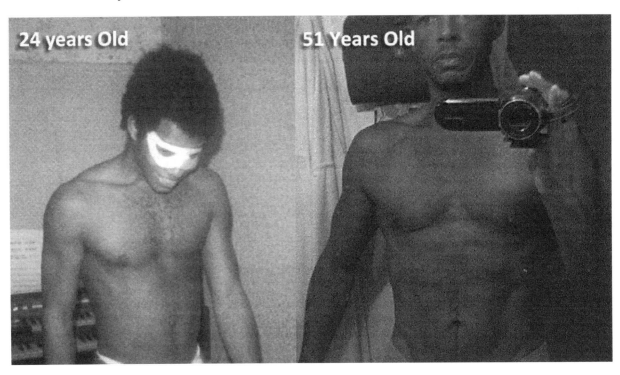

Comparing my body now and as it was 27 years earlier.

These last three years have been an amazing journey of discovery and adventure and this book is a compilation of everything I have learned in that time.

This book is not a scholarly work and is not intended to be, it is not based on a personal belief system but rather a profound knowing that comes as a result of exhaustive research, firsthand experience (so-called anecdotal evidence), the experiences of others (even more so-called anecdotal evidence) and intuition.

It is important to me to share this knowledge as not only is it life-changing and life-saving information but I believe it has much wider implications.

If you accept the principle of correspondence, that is,

"As above so below, as below so above"

And if you further accept that the exterior world is a reflection of your interior world then it would follow that the secret to healing the sickness that we see in the Earth around us, is to heal the pain and suffering within ourselves.

Allegedly Dave
www.allegedlydave.com
dave@allegedlydave.com

Testimonials

I have included a set of testimonials to the effectiveness of the approach to healing detailed in this book. All of the contributors are people I have interacted with, either personally or via social media, but unlike other testimonials I have encountered, which I have found frustrating because it is near impossible to verify or discuss the claims, I have included (with their permission of course) the email addresses of each of them.

* * * *

"Before I started this programme, I suffered from a long list of ailments including, Candida, Arthritis, aching armpits (lymph problems) including a tennis ball size lump under the left armpit, a severe lack of energy, irritable bowel syndrome, adrenal fatigue, constipation, migraines, tinnitus, severe brain fog, bloodshot eyes and yellow whites of eyes, greasy skin and hair and feelings of anger. Many of these things were brought on by an accident, in which I inhaled Arsenic.

I knew that this wouldn't be easy; there was poison in there which had to come out. The first week I experienced detox symptoms, I felt severe lethargy, sickness and diarrhoea, but then the headaches subsided almost immediately, my mood changed to more positive and much calmer and my skin looked younger and pores smaller.

By end of the second week I had lost about 10lbs in weight, I had much more energy, the tinnitus had subsided, the constipation and arthritis had gone, the lump under my arm had gone down to flat and my hair still looking clean after 3 Days rather than 6 Hours. Most importantly for me, my brain more agile again which seemed the most difficult thing to tackle. After 4 Weeks I had dropped a dress size.

If I'm honest I haven't been totally rigorous about this programme, but have still found fantastic results. I truly wish I'd known about this 14 Years ago when I first needed help. Out of all the many expensive treatments I have had, most have helped in some ways, but none of them has given me such dramatic results on every level.

Thank you so much Dave !! This has transformed my health and therefore my life."

Linda Brin
Shropshire, UK
linda.brin@hotmail.com

"In 2008, after I starting consuming a processed artificial sweetener containing Aspartame, I started experiencing an array of symptoms that were debilitating at times.

I was diagnosed as having IBS and Candida Albicans where I was suffering from food sensitivity's, and become sensitive to light, sounds, chemicals and my entire body was achy and weak. Desperate to regain my health, I tried a array of treatments, these included Homoeopathy, Pharmaceuticals drugs, Candida cleanse diet, Colonic irrigation, Acupuncture, Chinese herbal medicine, and many more with little or no positive effect.

I was deeply impressed following just one conversation with Dave about urine therapy and it was enough to kick start my healing journey, so it's a pleasure to write my testimonial for his book.

Consuming distilled water and urine has changed not only my physical and mental health but my entire outlook on life, health and skin care. I came to understand that pure water and or urine have the ability to restore unhealthy cells, not something I say lightly, but having experienced it myself and knowing of thousands of people around the globe who are having the same experience, I feel confident to share this information.

It was just 48 hours after I started Urine Therapy that I had lost 3lb in weight, which commonly happens as the toxins in the body are stored as fluid, and distilled water draws all the inorganic toxic minerals out, so the water retention drops. My very stubborn Dermatitis on my hand, which the GP had prescribed steroid cream for while advising it was the 'only treatment' that would cure it, was almost completely gone within four days. My IBS symptoms are getting better every day, while my skin is as soft as it's ever been.

All round I'm experiencing the ill effects in the body simply melting away like no other medication or product has even come close to in comparison; Having 14 years combined experience in the Holistic / Beauty Industry and 8 in the Health Care Industry, that's quite something to say, but every level of my physical, mental and emotional body are changing for the better; my energy has increased and a sense of aliveness, well being and contentment is experienced, which I am deep grateful for every day.

Thank you Dave for your bravery in talking about this well needed topic."

Trinity Jordan,
Milton Keynes, UK
Itstartshere.me@hotmail.com

"Hi Dave, I think it's wonderful that you have written a book about Urine Therapy and Distilled Water. I have been using this miracle alternative for a year now and I'm so happy with the results.

I do both urine therapy and distilled water it has given me energy and I no longer have anaemia (no pills) it has treated the fatty liver I had and it is so relaxing that its treating my anxiety little by little day by day.

I also rub urine all over my body and face every night until morning, it leaves skin so soft and it got rid of an age spot on my face and my stretch marks from child birth many years ago are starting to fade. I'm 46 years old and many people mistake my 27 year old son as my boyfriend/brother which he totally hates lol.

I first heard about urine therapy from my cousin Lily from Mexico who was going through advanced uterus cancer. She was at her doctor's office all depressed after the doctor told her that her only chance was chemotherapy and radiation therapy. She did not want to go through all that, a nurse from that same clinic that became good friends with her told her about urine therapy and told her not to mention it to anyone there or she'll lose her job. In my cousin's desperate situation she fasted on only urine and distilled water for a week and then only urine for 30 days she started to feel better and her energy was returned. .She then juiced raw veggies with continued urine therapy and distilled water for another month. When she went back to the doctor, he was surprised that she missed her appointment for chemotherapy 37 days earlier, but he was shocked to see the new x - rays that she had no more cancer!

I'm so grateful to know about miracles of our own perfect medicine. . Please feel free use my story if you want... God bless you."

Jessica M. Baros-Pineda
Norwalk, California
jessiemiles23@yahoo.com

"I have been on the therapies for about 2 months, I have noticed many things, my skin is no longer dry and looks healthier, blemishes disappear quicker and I'm getting less of them. I was getting those man hair growing on my chin and now they've gone, there is less gray in my hair, it's much healthier and fuller with less dryness on ends. I also think my eyesight has improved, but I'm not 100% sure on that one.

I was on anti-depressants for 25 years and now I'm off and never ever felt better in my life!"

Mia Spacee
Oscoda, Michigan
mia.spase@gmail.com

"My daughter AnnaJoy is mentally as well as physically disabled, so although she is now 23, she is still a "child" and has been in diapers for 21 years. She was incontinent due to Cerebral Palsy and could not stay dry more than 10 minutes. She had constant bladder infections and ended up with e-coli in her bladder, thus the cranberry juice was most of her fluid intake.

At the beginning of 2012 I found the book "The Water of Life" by John Armstrong and I believed urine therapy could help my daughter. She is adopted so we do not share the same DNA but I had read somewhere that nature is so loving that those who live in the same household carry what each other needs in their own body/urine.

Since she was in diapers I could not collect her urine so I started putting shot glasses of my own urine in her cranberry juice every day.

After 2 months of me hiding shot glasses of my urine in her cranberry juice, her bladder was healed. After 4 months her bowels were healed. She has been diaper free since spring of 2012 thanks to urine therapy.

Blessings"

Rayla Daniels
Corpus Christie, Texas
9pentacles@gmail.com

"I have had juvenile diabetes for 44 years, I got it when I was 10 years old. Distilled Waters are saving my life and reversing the damage that has been done by sugar running around in my blood for so long.

I was aging faster inside than people my own age. I was dehydrating slowly but surely.

It's been over 2 years of drinking my own water every day and supplementing with machine made distilled water. For the first time in my life I am hydrated and healing.

The healing started instantly from the very first day of drinking my own water.

Today my glycoslated haemoglobin Hgb A1c is the lowest it's ever been in the 44 years of experiencing this disease (6.3). This is sure sign that what I'm doing is the truth for me. My eyes, lungs, heart, kidneys, nerves, bones and joints are healing and so much more that it is hard to describe. With the physical healing comes emotional healing and this leaves me peaceful and positive about the future."

Anna Hilde Smith
Danville, California
hildesmith@Comcast.net

"I'd been suffering from chronic neck pain for about seven years. I'd tried massage, change of diet, exercises, but although the symptoms were sometimes more severe than at other times, nothing really relieved the pain. It was the kind of pain that meant I found it difficult to turn my neck beyond approximately 2 o'clock and 10 o'clock. I eventually went to see a chiropractor but was unimpressed with the results.

On January 4th 2014 I began looping my own urine, eating nothing and drinking nothing but distilled water. It was an interesting journey. I'm very slim and I lost a lot of weight which is an unfortunate side effect, but within a few days my neck was pain free.

Also, within a couple of weeks of beginning urine therapy my fingernails which had been weak and easily torn for years suddenly became tough as nails!

I have done two urine fasts that were each two days long, drinking all the urine I produced. About a week or two after the second fast I noticed that a small lump (benign tumour?) that was about the size of a small pea implanted under the skin on my calf had disappeared. It had been there for twenty years and I'd never known what it was. I still have the small patch of dark skin where it used to be.

Since my New Year urine fast, I have experienced another interesting thing. For the last approximately five years I had suffered from a recurring 'sickness' that always followed the same pattern. Around midday I'd get a bit of a headache which would get worse as the day went on until by the evening I'd feel pretty sick and nauseous with no appetite. It was something like flu/fever symptoms and always by the next morning it was gone. I used to jokingly call it my 'time of the month' as it seemed to happen every few weeks. Most often it happened after a day working outdoors on a market, summer or winter, but I haven't had a single occurrence since this fast.

I drink my first passing every morning and plan to do more fasts."

Jake Fern
Brighton, UK
jake@hollowmoon.co.uk

"I had an unknown growth on the back of my neck spreading into my spine. I suffered with this lump for 5 months making the side of my face numb, the doctors weren't too hot on diagnosing it correctly so I ended up peeing on a medical bandage then wrapping it round my neck. And after just that one day of UT I got the feeling back in my face and within a week it was all gone."

Scottstein Jenkins
Pontypool, UK
sjreble@hotmail.com

*"I have been on one of the therapies since April and two of them since November, on a previous visit to the doctor my left eye was 20/30 and my right eye 20/100 with Cataracts blocking vision in the right and little ones in the left.   Today, left eye is now 20/25 and the right eye is 20/30 and **NO CATARACTS**!*

I have had a big cataract near the centre of the eye since I was a teen and now it's gone. My poor doctor was so confused he was stuttering.

I have been into fasting, herbs, juicing, healing, you name it since the 1980's.   Nothing beats these therapies, nothing.

I drink a gallon of distilled waters every day no matter what I eat. (or more!) I eat 80% Fruit and try to stay raw...but make allowances for social events...as long as it's vegan/or vegetarian...no meat no dairy no eggs if I can get around it.   I also use urine in my hair, eyes, skin and others, but key here is a gallon of distilled water a day, and give it time.   I have been on a gallon a day since last April.

I have practiced urine therapy off and on since 1999 and distilled water longer but did not connect the two or the importance of a gallon a day until April when I stumbled upon Andrew Norton Webber. I have been looping my urine since November along with a lot of fruit and juices and distilled waters pretty much every day.

I noticed a change in my vision in December...but it got worse first! Real blurry and then a week later it was crystal clear...not perfect but so happy!

I have been into fasting, herbs, juicing, healing, you name it I have done it since 1980ish.   Nothing beats urine therapy, nothing.   But just distilled water is a very close second."

Chey Thomas
Cameron Park, California
cheykaythomas@facebook.com

"Two days ago, my husband and I went with our niece and nephew to have a day out in the snow, playing and sliding down a huge hill. My husband had a little accident and fell down, damaging his ankle.

When we got home the pain was unbearable and his ankle was very swollen... he thought he had probably broken something... it didn't look very good. I immediately wrapped his whole foot in cotton wool, which I had previously soaked in very old urine, and I covered everything in saran wrap, to hold the urine packs in place and prevent the urine from leaking. Then I put a thick warm sock over his foot and wrapped it additionally in a very warm blanket. I intuitively felt that it was important to keep it hot, in order to allow more energy & blood circulation, plus also help the old urine to go through his skin.

After only 10 minutes the pain had completely gone down!!! And my husband could finally fall asleep.

The next day, his foot was almost completely back to normal! He was SO AMAZED to see this quick recovery!! He could barely believe it!

The pain is almost absolutely gone now and the swelling as well. He can even walk normally!! I've wrapped his foot again this evening, so he can still get the healing effects of the old urine during his night sleep and I'll do this a last third time tomorrow, just to be sure that it's all healed perfectly.

I think life gave him this experience, for him to see the healing powers of urine... or maybe it was my wish coming true.

Even though he loves and supports 100% my practice and also joins me doing it, he had not been such a believer as I am, simply because he didn't had the opportunity to test it for himself in a way that he could clearly see the benefits of it.

Now he is definitely a BELIEVER!!"

Mónica Schütt
Basel, Switzerland
monicanga@icloud.com

"When I first started out on 4 litres of distilled water, my throat immediately got really sore for a week or more. Before that time I was prone to bad throats, sometimes leading to colds. But since then I haven't had a bad throat for over a year, and only got a cold once for just 2 days.

Considering I travel frequently on planes, often the cause of the problem, I think this is really awesome, I'll be on the plane surrounded by all sorts of wheezing people and I just know I won't get sick! Also if I am in a smoky bar I don't get affected like before."

Oliver Langton
Sofia, Bulgaria
oliver_langton@yahoo.co.uk

"I have been doing the urine therapy for about a year now. I began and became inspired by watching some you-tube videos of both Andrew Norton Webber and Allegedly Dave. Interestingly, I had attempted to do urine therapy about ten years ago after reading a very inspiring book on it, but did not continue due to some unanswered questions about old urine and what was ok to drink. This time, I emailed Dave and this little bit of personal contact made the difference! He answered my questions in detail and also gave some very wonderful advice and insights. A lot of this has to do with food and our need for it, and the ability the body has to go without and to actually thrive.

This insight of imagining myself as a sculpture inside of a block of stone, exactly as I wish myself to be, strong and healthy, vibrant full of life energy made me really feel I could do it. I immediately gave up all cooked grains, chips and ate only raw food from then on, in addition to the urine therapy. As a runner, I really, really need my vital energy and am so aware of how I feel. The thing I really love about the urine therapy is that it completely makes sense to me. It is our own personal holographic imprint of everything going on in the body, distilled by our kidneys, and recycled. If there are any issues with the body such as parasites, yeast, or anything, this recycling action will signal the body to heal of that condition. I also believe to simultaneously withdraw food and let the body heal and rest is important too.

*I don't think one can do urine therapy for any length of time and **not** begin to question what we are putting in our bodies three times a day as food. If you eat or drink something that your body dislikes, immediately you can taste it in the urine. You will not want to eat or drink that thing again. Raw food still needs to take vital energy to digest, but at least it is full of enzymes and life. the cooked food is just addiction, and it is hard to monitor how much you are eating because it is dead food. it really is just for taste and comfort. When I would eat cooked rice or quinoa for a meal I would eat far more that needed because it just tasted good. Now that I eat raw, I eat really only how much I need, so my body and mind are more relaxed and have more energy for other things. The other thing I love about the urine therapy is that it keeps you alkaline. Since i have tried cleansing and fasting starting ten years ago never was my PH alkaline. It was always 5.0 (bright yellow), and could not be made alkaline no matter what. Now because of the urine the PH strip is always very green and alkaline and all body processes work better in alkaline environment.*

So I cannot say enough about this lifestyle. I believe if anyone digs deep enough they will find this is the way to go. I am still learning and drinking in information to improve myself in every way, and I am so thankful to Dave for giving me the impetus to continue!"

Sheri Culver
Cheyenne, Wyoming
Shericulver5@gmail.com

"Reading the book "Water of Life" by John Armstrong was my initiation into the urine therapy and I always wanted to do a long fast, like the ones depicted in the book, but I found myself so emotionally dependent on food that I struggled even to finish a day without any meal! After several attempts I finally did a 14 day fast! I drank all my urine plus some water, if needed, and did 1 to 3 times daily whole body massages with aged urine (2 to 5 years old) for 30 to 60 minutes each session.

The first week of the fast was like Hell.

I was constantly sneezing and coughing. A ton of mucus came out of my respiratory tract. My mouth was covered with plaque all the time and I had a headache that didn't stop. I became so weak I could barely speak or lift myself out of bed, but I gathered every day all the strength left in me to go to the bathroom and follow my drinking and massaging routine. All I could do was pee, drink, sleep, massage, shower and repeat.

A very deep healing took place on all levels of my being. The detox was not only physical, but also emotional and spiritual. Old past traumas, childhood memories, stored anger and resentment came to the surface and I had several meltdowns, crying my soul out for 3-5 minutes and then having the most liberating deep laughter and a state of joy and freedom followed. It was amazing! This turned out to be a total reboot of my whole being!

I dropped all the negative weight that I was carrying in my body, heart and soul. I lost about 11 kilos during that first week. I went from 54 kilos to 43 kilos. My face looked scary, like from a horror movie. My cheeks were gone, my eyelids were completely sunken, but something incredible happened... when I looked into my eyes... I saw the whole universe. My true self began to slowly reveal itself to me and all I could think was: "Wow, I am so beautiful". The universe was opening itself to me... I saw the window to my soul. It was as if with each day into the fast, I was cleaning more and more the glasses of that window and being able to look much deeper into me... into the whole universe! I get now tears in my eyes when I think of it. That gave me the strength to continue... even though I was in a lot of pain, extremely weak and my overall external appearance was that of a 3 day old corpse! I could see the light at the end of the tunnel.

As for physical healing: I thought that after being 3 years 85-95% raw vegan and drinking my urine daily, I was pretty much in perfect health. Well, I was wrong. On day 2 of the fast, a cyst I had on my upper right shoulder started coming out. (I wasn't much aware of it, only at times, when it was itching or hurting and I kind of got used to the numbness on that area) my skin opened itself right there on that spot and liquid started pouring out. I was so happy to see this immediate sign of healing and cleansing! Another cyst I had in my right ovary also got dissolved and now I no longer have any menstrual pain, which had been the curse of my life for the past 25 years! I could feel how my body was intensively working on those two areas and also on my kidneys, heart, brain and liver. My wrinkles also disappeared, but not completely, I feel that a longer fast is needed to fully regenerate the skin. It's a process that takes a bit more time, but now continuing with the daily urine massages I can see a big improvement!

The second week of the fast was like heaven. I started slowly gaining back my energy and having moments of pure joy. They were fleeting in the beginning, coming and going, and later became a constant. I started having the most amazing 3D visions, especially during the night, and not only in dreams but also while being fully awake! In fact, I couldn't sleep much at all. I slept in intervals of 2 hours. Instead of sleeping I was more like in a trance during the night, watching these amazing 3D movies. I also experienced wonderful interaction and communication with my cells. They were extremely happy to receive my attention. It was one of the most wonderful experiences I had! I could feel what my cells feel, I clearly felt the oneness with them and understood it is a perfect reflection of the macrocosm in the microcosm. I knew that for them having me talk to them or just focusing my attention on them was if like GOD finally had spoken to them. They were so happy and thrilled about that interaction with me. I thanked them wholeheartedly for all the amazing work they were doing and felt that they were dancing and singing, making a party inside my body, because finally I had spoken to them.

We are so not alone in our own bodies... we have millions of friends!!! I am so blessed, we are all so blessed, we come into this world already with a billion best friends that are here for us and will do everything for us!!

My mind also became so clear, I could think of any subject with the sharpest intelligence and insight... I was having the deepest conversations with myself, with my soul, with this higher intelligence in me. I feel like I began to activate and use the dormant part of my brain and that I was also activating the dormant DNA in me. I was consciously directing my cells into what they should do.

On day 9. I felt my whole body being almost 100% pure and free of any obstacle (toxins, impurities) and I felt a rush of energy moving through me, coming from all directions of the universe and also from inside my heart. I almost jumped out of my bed! I felt like singing and dancing! I was like in ecstasy and this feeling continued, it became more and more intense. From that moment on, real "miracles" started happening...

That second week I gained all the weight I had lost. I went from being 43 kilos to 55 kilos! In just a matter of days, I had put on the 11 kilos I had lost and gained an additional one!! It was really incredible for me to experience this. I could almost watch my body, my muscles, my tissues growing in front of me! It was amazing!

On day 13 I probably experienced what people would call a "kundalini" awakening or the beginning of one. I saw myself as a ball of light, the brightest light you can imagine and I sunk into it. I felt like exploding and imploding at the same time into that ball of light. It was a marvelous feeling, but at the same time the most frightening one. I can't really put it in words. It lasted only the blink of an eye, because I stopped it. I kind of forced myself to "come back into my body". I screamed, just to "connect" back to the physical. I was afraid that I would disintegrate and disappear. My mind was not ready to completely let go. My ego was yelling "Don't kill me!!" (literally! I think that my ego or past identifications were one step away from dissolving into the new real me). I decided that I wanted to take a break and postpone the experience of "enlightenment" for some time.

About 3 months later I felt ready to take on the deeper journey into myself and started another urine fast. Very quickly I found myself back on the same level of awareness as before. On day 4 I had this experience again but this time I just let it happen. I took the step and what came afterwards was so amazingly mind-blowing that I couldn't do it justice. All I will share now is that I was in Nirvana for about 15 hours... I met my true self and I knew all there is to know about everything. I was just pure consciousness. That's what we all are.

Thank you for allowing me to share my story here."

Mónica Schütt
Basel, Switzerland
monicanga@icloud.com

Repairs and Overhaul

Troubleshooting

As previously explained, all so-called disease begins as a thought pattern that causes an emotional response weakening or causing imbalances in the body. The body responds by healing or eliminating, which is what the allopathic establishment calls "symptoms of disease".

As I started to catalogue the specific mental and emotional patterns that are the cause of these symptoms, I found that this task had already been performed in minute detail by **Louise L. Hay**.

In this section I rely heavily upon her research as it is an integral part of the healing process and ongoing preventative care. However, if you would like to know more about the direct connection between thought patterns and the manifestation of disease, and how to reprogramming those thought patterns then I would strongly suggest you read **Louise L. Hay's** utterly amazing book "*You Can Heal Your Life*".

The following is a reference guide to common ailments that can be healed by the holistic approach of addressing the mental, emotional and physical aspects of illness.

The physical healing techniques listed for each of these ailments will be very similar to each other because, despite the plethora of diseases, ailments and disorders that have been invented by the medical mafia, there are only two states that the human body exists in, and they are "good health" and "bad health." Thus there is only one method of healing the human body and that is to stay out of the way of the body's natural healing abilities and use natural means to assist it to eliminate toxins.

How to use this reference guide

First, look up the entry that most closely matches the ailment in question. This listing is far from a complete listing however, since the method of treatment is non-medicinal and consists of allowing the body to heal itself without interference. The treatment of an illness not listed can be inferred from the methods employed for other similar illnesses.

Examine the associated thought pattern trigger and emotional response and determine whether these or similar thoughts and emotions apply.

Apply the processes detailed in the physical healing section, referring to the appropriate appendices as directed. The physical healing processes below will appear similar but that is because, as noted earlier, there are no such things as distinct illnesses and diseases only bad health and it only requires the combination of very few therapies and practices to aid the body in restoring good health.

Whenever you experience such thoughts and emotions then rewrite this subconscious programming with the mantra in the thought pattern reprogramming section.

For detailed information about how to reprogram mental and emotional thought patterns, please refer to the book *"You Can Heal Your Life"* **by Louise L. Hay.**

Reference Guide

Acne

Thought pattern trigger:

"I hate myself, I am ugly"

Emotional response:

Self loathing.

Physical Healing

Pour a small amount of either fresh or aged urine into the palm of the hand and massage lightly into the affected area, making sure that the area is well saturated, and continue to massage until the urine has completely absorbed into the skin. Reapply as many times as desired, the more the area is treated in this way the better.

If the acne is severe then saturate a clean cotton pad with aged urine, place on the affected area and secure in place with a gauze or cotton wrap, keep wet with additional applications of aged urine.

Also, consider changing diet to one to two small meals of mostly organic juicy fruits, berries, nuts or leafy green salads (avoiding fibrous "earthy" vegetables) and distilled water or freshly squeezed juice.

Thought pattern reprogramming:

"I love and accept myself, I am beautiful"

Aids

Thought pattern trigger:

"There's nothing I can do about it. No one would care if I lived or died."

Emotional response:

Denial of the self, inadequacy, sexual guilt.

Physical Healing

Perform an enema containing about a half litre of fresh or aged urine warmed to body temperature in order to cleanse the bowels.

Begin a course of urine therapy by collecting the first urination of the morning midstream and then again late in the afternoon or early evening. The frequency of urine drinking should be slowly increased until every urination passed is drunk. (**see Appendix I**) Night time urinations should be saved for urine massages.

Drink distilled water to bring the combined water and urine intake to approximately four litres per day. (**see Appendix II**)

Observe a two day fast each week, that is, consume no food for those days only drink urine and distilled water, after 3 – 4 weeks fast for one week each month.

Depending on the severity of the symptoms a complete fast should be observed for between fourteen and thirty days, during this time only urine and distilled water should be given to drink, and **absolutely no food whatsoever**.

Rest, rest, rest.

Thought pattern reprogramming:

"I am part of the Universal design. I am important and I am loved by Life itself. I am powerful and capable. I love and appreciate all of myself."

Alcoholism

Thought pattern trigger:

"What's the point? I give up."

Emotional response:

Futility, guilt, inadequacy, self rejection.

Physical Healing

Begin urine therapy by collecting the first urination of the morning, midstream, and drink within fifteen minutes of collection. Save a little of the urine to massage into the body. Repeat the process in the late afternoon or early evening. (**see Appendix I**)

Drink distilled water to bring the combined water and urine intake to approximately four litres per day. (**see Appendix II**)

Thought pattern reprogramming:

"I live in the now, every moment is a new opportunity to improve. I love and approve of myself, I am worth it."

Allergies

Thought pattern trigger:

"Who are you allergic to?"

Emotional response:

Fear, guilt, powerless.

Physical Healing

Change diet to one to two small meals of juicy fruits and or light leafy green salads and fast two days per week, these need not be consecutive days.

Begin urine therapy by collecting the first urination of the morning, midstream, and drink within fifteen minutes of collection. Save a little of the urine to massage into the body. Repeat the process in the late afternoon or early evening. (**see Appendix I**)

Drink distilled water to bring the combined water and urine intake to approximately four litres per day. (**see Appendix II**)

If allergic reactions occur, wait 10 – 15 seconds after the appearance of symptoms, collect urine and place 10 drops of urine under the tongue and hold it there for as long as possible, repeat until all symptoms subside

Alternatively, a homeopathic solution can be prepared from urine collected at the height of an allergic reaction (**see Appendix I**)

Thought pattern reprogramming:

"The world is safe and friendly. I am safe. I am at peace with life."

Alzheimer's Disease

Thought pattern trigger:

"Refusal to deal with the world as it is. Escapism."

Emotional response:

Hopelessness, helplessness and anger.

Physical Healing

Change diet to that which includes fruit smoothies made with **Coriander** and **Chlorella** two to three times a day, and small infrequent meals of juicy fruits, nuts or light leafy greens and distilled water.

Begin urine therapy by collecting the first urination of the morning, midstream, and drink within fifteen minutes of collection. Save a little of the urine to massage into the body. Repeat the process in the late afternoon or early evening. (**see Appendix I**)

Drink distilled water to bring the combined water and urine intake to approximately four litres per day. (**see Appendix II**)

The physical cause of Alzheimer's disease, dementia and senility can be traced to heavy metal poisoning. Coriander stimulates the release of these heavy metals lodged in the brain as well as the other organs and tissues, and Chlorella helps conduct the metal particles from the bloodstream to the liver where they are excreted via the bowels.

Thought pattern reprogramming:

"There is always a new and better way for me to experience life. I forgive and release the past. I move into joy."

Anemia

Thought pattern trigger:

"Yes-but..." attitude.

Emotional response:

Joylessness, fear, inadequacy.

Physical Healing

Change diet to one to two small meals of juicy fruits, nuts or light leafy green salads and fast two days per week, these need not be consecutive days.

Begin urine therapy by collecting the first urination of the morning, midstream, and drink within fifteen minutes of collection. Save a little of the urine to massage into the body. Repeat the process in the late afternoon or early evening. (**see Appendix I**)

Drink distilled water to bring the combined water and urine intake to approximately four litres per day. (**see Appendix II**)

If symptoms of Anemia persist after four weeks then start a thirty day urine fast. In other words, take no food during that period, only drink all urine passed and distilled water up to four litres a day.

Thought pattern reprogramming:

"It is safe for me to experience joy in every area of my life. I love life."

Appendicitis

Thought pattern trigger:

"This is scary, nothing good can come from this."

Emotional response:

Fear.

Physical Healing

Complete bed rest.

Begin urine therapy by collecting the first urination of the morning midstream and drink within fifteen minutes of collection, save a little of the urine to massage into the body. Repeat the process in the late afternoon or early evening. (**see Appendix I**)

Only drink distilled water and urine, eat **no food** whatsoever for three days, fruit juices may be taken from the third day onward.

Place a urine pack over the painful area, secure in place with cling film and keep wet with regular applications of urine until the acute symptoms subside.

After the acute symptoms subside, by about the third day, perform an enema containing about a half litre of body temperature urine once a day until the inflammation and pain have subsided.

Change diet to small infrequent meals of juicy fruits, nuts or light leafy greens and fast two days per week, these need not be consecutive days.

Thought pattern reprogramming:

"I am safe, I relax and let life flow joyously."

Anorexia

Thought pattern trigger:

"Denying the self."

Emotional response:

Extreme fear

Physical Healing

Begin urine therapy by collecting the first urination of the morning midstream and drink within fifteen minutes of collection, save a little of the urine to massage into the body. Repeat the process in the late afternoon or early evening. (**see Appendix I**)

Change diet to one to two small meals of juicy fruits, nuts or light leafy green salads (raw salads with no dressing and avoiding fibrous and "earthy" vegetables) and fast two days per week, these need not be consecutive days.

Thought pattern reprogramming:

"It is safe to be me. I am wonderful just as I am. I choose to live. I choose joy and self-acceptance."

Anxiety

Thought pattern trigger:

"Not trusting the flow and the process of life."

Emotional response:

Fear, worry.

Physical Healing

Begin urine therapy by collecting the first urination of the morning midstream and drink within fifteen minutes of collection, save a little of the urine to massage into the body. Repeat the process in the late afternoon or early evening. (**see Appendix I**)

Drink distilled water to bring the combined water and urine intake to approximately four litres per day. (**see Appendix II**)

Change diet to small infrequent meals of juicy fruits, nuts or light leafy greens and fast two days per week, these need not be consecutive days. Completely avoid sugar, meat, dairy products, bread, cakes, biscuits and other processed foods. Drink only urine and distilled water.

Thought pattern reprogramming:

"I love and approve of myself and I trust the process of life. I am safe ."

Arteriosclerosis

Thought pattern trigger:

"It's impossible, it can't be done, those others don't know what they are talking about.."

Emotional response:

Tension, narrow-mindedness.

Physical Healing

Begin urine therapy by collecting the first midstream urination of the morning and drink within fifteen minutes of collection, save a little of the urine to massage into the body. Repeat the process in the late afternoon or early evening. (**see Appendix I**)

Drink distilled water to bring the combined water and urine intake to approximately four litres per day. (**see Appendix II**)

Fast on urine and distilled water for five to seven days, that is, **eat no food whatsoever**.

During the period of fasting, perform daily enemas with a half litre to a litre of fresh urine (aged urine may also be used) warmed to body temperature or mixed with warm distilled water.

After the fast, resume eating one or two small meals daily of fresh juicy fruits, berries, nuts and seeds or light leafy green salads (raw salads with no dressing avoiding fibrous "earthy" vegetables) Also, continue to fast for two days every week, these need not be consecutive days.

Thought pattern reprogramming:

"I am completely open to life and to joy. I choose to see with love"

Arthritis

Thought pattern trigger:

"Feeling unloved. Criticism, resentment"

Emotional response:

Feeling unloved, resentment.

Physical Healing

Perform an enema containing about a half litre of fresh or aged urine warmed to body temperature in order to cleanse the bowels.

Begin urine therapy by collecting the first urination of the morning midstream and drink within fifteen minutes of collection, save a little of the urine to massage into the body. Repeat the process in the late afternoon or early evening. (**see Appendix I**) Night time urinations should be saved for urine massages.

During urine massages give extra attention to swollen joints, if swellings are painful then use a urine pack on the site of the swelling (**see Appendix I**)

Urine should be supplemented with Distilled water to bring the combined water and urine intake to approximately four litres per day. (**see Appendix II**)

Depending on the severity of the symptoms a complete fast should be observed for between three and thirty days, during this time only urine and distilled water should be given to drink, and **absolutely no food whatsoever**.

Rest, rest, rest.

Thought pattern reprogramming:

"I am love. I now choose to love and approve of myself. I see others with love."

Asthma

Thought pattern trigger:

Smother love. Inability to breathe for one's self.

Emotional response:

Feeling stifled, suppressed grief.

Physical Healing

Perform an enema containing about a half litre of fresh or aged urine warmed to body temperature in order to cleanse the bowels.

Begin a course of urine therapy by collecting the first midstream urination of the morning and then again late in the afternoon or early evening, (**see Appendix I**) the frequency of urine drinking can be slowly increased until all daytime urine passed is drunk. Night time urinations should be saved for urine massages.

Urine should be supplemented with Distilled water to bring the combined water and urine intake to approximately four litres per day. (**see Appendix II**)

Depending on the severity of the symptoms a complete fast should be observed for between three and thirty days, during this time only urine and distilled water should be given to drink, and **absolutely no food whatsoever**.

Rest, rest, rest.

Thought pattern reprogramming:

"It is safe now for me to take charge of my own life. I choose to be free."

Back Problems

Thought pattern trigger:

"I can't do this on my own… I've had this for so long… Get off my back."

Emotional response:

Feeling unloved, guilt, fear.

Physical Healing

Begin urine therapy. Drink the first midstream urination of the morning within fifteen minutes of collection, saving a little of the urine to massage into the body. Repeat the process in the late afternoon or early evening. (**see Appendix I**)

Drink distilled water to bring the combined water and urine intake to approximately four litres per day. (**see Appendix II**)

Use a urine pack on the painful area of the back. Saturate a clean cotton pad or a clean folded cloth with aged urine, place on the affected area and secure in place with cling film or a gauze, keep wet with additional applications of aged urine.

Thought pattern reprogramming:

"I release the past. I am free to move forward. Life supports and loves me. I love and approve of myself."

Bladder Problems

Thought pattern trigger:

"Holding on to old ideas. Fear of letting go. Being pissed off."

Emotional response:

Anxiety.

Physical Healing

Begin urine therapy. Drink the first midstream urination of the morning within fifteen minutes of collection, saving a little of the urine to massage into the body. Repeat the process in the late afternoon or early evening. (**see Appendix I**)

Drink distilled water, optionally mixed with freshly squeezed lemon or lime, to bring the combined water and urine intake to approximately four litres per day. (**see Appendix II**)

Thought pattern reprogramming:

"I comfortably and easily release the old and welcome the new in my life. I am safe."

Blood Pressure (High)

Thought pattern trigger:

"Long-standing unsolved emotional problem"

Emotional response:

Tension.

Physical Healing

Begin urine therapy. Drink the first midstream urination of the morning within fifteen minutes of collection, saving a little of the urine to massage into the body. Repeat the process in the late afternoon or early evening. (**see Appendix I**)

Drink distilled water to bring the combined water and urine intake to approximately four litres per day. (**see Appendix II**)

Thought pattern reprogramming:

"I joyously release the past. I am at peace."

Blood Pressure (Low)

Thought pattern trigger:

"What's the use? It won't work anyway."

Emotional response:

Lack of love as a child, defeatism.

Physical Healing

Begin urine therapy. Drink the first midstream urination of the morning within fifteen minutes of collection, saving a little of the urine to massage into the body. Repeat the process in the late afternoon or early evening. (**see Appendix I**)

Drink distilled water to bring the combined water and urine intake to approximately four litres per day. (**see Appendix II**)

Thought pattern reprogramming:

"I now choose to live in the ever-joyous NOW. My life is a joy.."

Bowel Problems

Thought pattern trigger:

"I need that, I can't leave it behind."

Emotional response:

Fear of letting go of the old and no longer needed.

Physical Healing

Begin urine therapy. Drink the first midstream urination of the morning within fifteen minutes of collection, saving a little of the urine to massage into the body. Repeat the process in the late afternoon or early evening. (**see Appendix I**)

Drink distilled water to bring the combined water and urine intake to approximately four litres per day. (**see Appendix II**)

Fast on urine and distilled water for 5 – 7 days, that is, **eat no food whatsoever**.

During the period of fasting, perform daily enemas with a half litre to a litre of aged urine (fresh urine may also be used) warmed to body temperature or mixed with warm distilled water.

After the fast, resume eating one or two small meals daily of fresh juicy fruits, berries, nuts and seeds or light leafy green salads (raw salads with no dressing avoiding fibrous "earthy" vegetables) Also, continue to fast for two days every week, these need not be consecutive days.

Thought pattern reprogramming:

"I freely and easily release the old and joyously welcome the new."

Breast Problems - *Cysts, Lumps, Mastitis*

Thought pattern trigger:

"I'm not important... my children come first.."

Emotional response:

Overmothering, overprotective attitudes.

Physical Healing

Begin urine therapy. Drink the first midstream urination of the morning within fifteen minutes of collection, saving a little of the urine to massage into the body, paying particular attention to the chest area. Repeat the process in the late afternoon or early evening. (**see Appendix I**)

Drink distilled water to bring the combined water and urine intake to approximately four litres per day. (**see Appendix II**)

Use a urine pack over the site of any cysts or lumps. Saturate a clean cotton pad or a clean folded cloth with preferably aged urine, place on the affected area and secure in place with cling film or a gauze, keep wet with additional applications of urine.

Consider changing the diet to one to two small meals of juicy fruits, nuts or light leafy green salads (raw salads with no dressing and avoiding fibrous and "earthy" vegetables) and fast two days per week, these need not be consecutive days.

Thought pattern reprogramming:

"I am important. I count. I now care for and nourish myself with love and with joy. I allow others the freedom to be who they are. We are all safe and free."

Bronchitis

Thought pattern trigger:

Inflamed family environment. Arguments and yelling. Sometimes silent

Emotional response:

Grief, suppressed anger.

Physical Healing

Fast on urine and distilled water for two weeks. Eat no food whatsoever and drink all urine passed, do not perform any urine massages during this time. Drink distilled water to bring the combined water and urine intake to approximately four litres per day. (**see Appendix II**)

Break the fast by eating one or two small meals daily of fresh juicy fruits, berries, nuts and seeds or light leafy green salads (raw salads with no dressing and avoiding fibrous "earthy" vegetables) while continuing to consume urine twice a day and distilled water as required.

After a week, begin a series of 3 – 5 day urine and distilled water fasts, this time performing regular urine massages, paying particular attention to the chest area. Break the fasts with seven day periods of small meals as detailed above and continue this cycle until the symptoms have completely abated.

Improvement should be seen within three days, however this process should be continued at least to the end of the first 3 – 5 day fast.

Thought pattern reprogramming:

"I declare peace and harmony within me and around me. All is well."

Cancer

Thought pattern trigger:

"I've always hated him. What's the use?"

Emotional response:

Deep hurt, longstanding resentment, grief, hatred.

Physical Healing

Perform an enema containing about a half litre of fresh or aged urine warmed to body temperature in order to cleanse the bowels.

Begin a course of urine therapy by collecting the first urination of the morning midstream (**see Appendix I**) and then again late in the afternoon or early evening. The frequency of urine drinking should be slowly increased until every urination passed is drunk. Night time urinations should be saved for urine massages.

Drink oxygenated distilled water to bring the combined water and urine intake to approximately four litres per day. Distilled water can be oxygenated by following a hydrogen peroxide protocol, starting with 3 drops of 35% food grade hydrogen peroxide in a 250ml glass of distilled water 3 times a day, and increasing the dosage until a maintenance dosage of 25 drops is achieved (**see Appendix II**

Depending on the severity of the symptoms a complete fast should be observed for between three and thirty days, during this time only urine and oxygenated distilled water should be given to drink, and **absolutely no food whatsoever**.

Use a urine pack over the site of any cysts, lumps or sores. Saturate a clean cotton pad or a clean folded cloth with preferably aged urine, place on the affected area and secure in place with cling film or a gauze, keep wet with additional applications of urine.

Rest, rest, rest.

Thought pattern reprogramming:

"I lovingly forgive and release all of the past. I choose to fill my world with joy. I love and approve of myself."

Candida

Thought pattern trigger:

Feeling very scattered. Demanding and untrusting in relationships. Great takers.

Emotional response:

Frustration and anger

Physical Healing

Begin urine therapy. Drink the first midstream urination of the morning within fifteen minutes of collection, saving a little of the urine to massage into the body, paying particular attention to any area that have become symptomatic. Repeat the process in the late afternoon or early evening. (**see Appendix I**)

Drink distilled water to bring the combined water and urine intake to approximately four litres per day. (**see Appendix II**)

Thought pattern reprogramming:

"I give myself permission to be all that I can be, and I deserve the very best in life. I love and appreciate myself and others."

Cataracts

Thought pattern trigger:

Inability to see ahead with joy. Dark future.

Emotional response:

Dread, despair.

Physical Healing

Begin urine therapy. Drink the first midstream urination of the morning within fifteen minutes of collection. Save some urine to massage into the body, as well as enough to fill an eyewash cup. Bathe the eyes in urine, blinking fifty times and perhaps perform eye exercises

Repeat the process in the late afternoon or early evening. (**see Appendix I**)

Drink distilled water to bring the combined water and urine intake to approximately four litres per day. (**see Appendix II**)

Thought pattern reprogramming:

"Life is eternal and filled with joy. I look forward to every moment."

Cerebral Palsy

Thought pattern trigger:

"A need to unite the family in an action of love."

Emotional response:

Fear, terror.

Physical Healing

Perform an enema containing about a half litre of fresh or aged urine warmed to body temperature in order to cleanse the bowels.

Begin a course of urine therapy by collecting the first urination of the morning midstream (**see Appendix I**) and then again late in the afternoon or early evening. The frequency of urine drinking should be slowly increased until every urination passed is drunk.

Urine should be supplemented with distilled water up to a total liquid intake of four litres daily.

Night time urinations should be saved for urine massages.

Depending on the severity of the symptoms a complete fast should be observed for between three and thirty days. During this time only urine and distilled water should be given to drink, and **absolutely no food whatsoever**.

Rest, rest, rest.

Thought pattern reprogramming:

"I contribute to a united, loving, and peaceful family life. All is well."

Colon Problems

Thought pattern trigger:

"Fear of letting go. Holding on to the past."

Emotional response:

Fear, anxiety

Physical Healing

Begin urine therapy. Drink the first midstream urination of the morning within fifteen minutes of collection. Save some urine to massage into the body. Repeat the process in the late afternoon or early evening. **(see Appendix I)**

Drink distilled water to bring the combined water and urine intake to approximately four litres per day. **(see Appendix II)**

Perform an enema containing about a half litre of fresh or aged urine warmed to body temperature once a day for 3 – 5 days.

Thought pattern reprogramming:

"I easily release that which I no longer need. The past is over, and I am free."

Conjunctivitis

Thought pattern trigger:

"I hate seeing this.. I don't want to see..."

Emotional response:

Anger, frustration

Physical Healing

Begin urine therapy. Drink the first midstream urination of the morning within fifteen minutes of collection. Save some urine to massage into the body, as well as enough to fill an eyewash cup. Bathe the eyes in urine, blinking fifty times and perhaps perform eye exercises.

Repeat the process in the late afternoon or early evening. (**see Appendix I**)

Drink distilled water to bring the combined water and urine intake to approximately four litres per day. (**see Appendix II**)

Thought pattern reprogramming:

"I see with eyes of love. There is a harmonious solution, and I accept it now."

Constipation

Thought pattern trigger:

"Refusing to release old ideas. Stuck in the past. Sometimes stinginess."

Emotional response:

Fear, worry

Physical Healing

Begin urine therapy. Drink the first midstream urination of the morning within fifteen minutes of collection. Save some urine to massage into the body. Repeat the process in the late afternoon or early evening. (**see Appendix I**)

Drink distilled water to bring the combined water and urine intake to approximately four litres per day. (**see Appendix II**)

Perform an enema containing about a half litre of fresh or aged urine warmed to body temperature once a day for 3 – 5 days.

Thought pattern reprogramming:

"As I release the past, the new and fresh and vital enter. I allow life to flow through me."

Crohn's Disease

Thought pattern trigger:

"Fear of letting go. Holding on to the past."

Emotional response:

Fear, anxiety

Physical Healing

Perform an enema containing about a half litre of fresh or aged urine warmed to body temperature once a day for three to five days.

Begin a course of urine therapy by collecting the first urination of the morning midstream (**see Appendix I**) and then again late in the afternoon or early evening. As the days pass, the frequency of urine drinking should be slowly increased until every daytime urination passed is drunk.

Night time urinations should be saved for urine massages.

While consuming all passed urine, a complete fast should be observed for between fourteen and thirty days. During this time only urine and distilled water should be given to drink, and **absolutely no food whatsoever**.

If areas of painful, red and swollen skin appear then perform additional urine massages upon the affected areas. However, if they persist or joint pain is experienced then apply a urine pack. Saturate a clean cotton pad or a clean folded cloth with preferably aged urine, place on the affected area and secure in place with cling film or a gauze, keep wet with additional applications of urine. (**see Appendix I**)

If there is inflammation or irritation of the eyes, fill an eyewash cup with fresh urine and bathe the eyes in urine, blinking fifty times and perhaps perform eye exercises.

Thought pattern reprogramming:

"I easily release that which I no longer need. The past is over, and I am free."

163

Cystic Fibrosis

Thought pattern trigger:

"A strong belief that life won't work. Poor me."

Emotional response:

Self pity, depression.

Physical Healing

Perform an enema containing about a half litre of fresh or aged urine warmed to body temperature in order to cleanse the bowels.

Begin a course of urine therapy by collecting the first urination of the morning midstream (**see Appendix I**) and then again late in the afternoon or early evening, the frequency of urine drinking should be slowly increased until every urination passed is drunk.

Urine should be supplemented with distilled water up to a total liquid intake of four litres daily.

A complete fast should be observed for between ten and thirty days, during this time only urine and distilled water should be given to drink, and **absolutely no food whatsoever**.

If sinus problems are experienced then sniff several drops of urine into the nostrils three times a day until these symptoms subside.

Thought pattern reprogramming:

"Life loves me, and I love life. I now choose to take in life fully and freely."

Deafness

Thought pattern trigger:

"I don't want to hear this. Don't bother me."

Emotional response:

Rejection, stubbornness, isolation.

Physical Healing

Pour a little fresh urine into the ears and stop the ears with cotton balls dipped in coconut oil to prevent leakage.

Begin urine therapy. Drink the first midstream urination of the morning within fifteen minutes of collection, saving a little of the urine to massage into the body, paying particular attention to the chest area. Repeat the process in the late afternoon or early evening. (**see Appendix I**)

Thought pattern reprogramming:

"I listen to the Divine and rejoice at all that I am able to hear. I am one with all."

Depression

Thought pattern trigger:

"I know I shouldn't be angry but..."

Emotional response:

Anger, hopelessness.

Physical Healing

Begin urine therapy by collecting the first urination of the morning midstream and drink within fifteen minutes of collection. Save a little of the urine to massage into the body. Repeat the process in the late afternoon or early evening. (**see Appendix I**)

Drink distilled water to bring the combined water and urine intake to approximately four litres per day. (**see Appendix II**)

Change diet to small infrequent meals of juicy fruits, nuts or light leafy greens and fast two days per week (these need not be consecutive days). Completely avoid sugar, meat, dairy products, bread, cakes, biscuits and other processed foods. Drink only urine and distilled water.

Thought pattern reprogramming:

"I now go beyond other people's fears and limitations. I create my life."

Diabetes

Thought pattern trigger:

Longing for what might have been. A great need to control. "No sweetness left."

Emotional response:

Deep sorrow.

Physical Healing

Perform an enema containing about a half litre of fresh or aged urine warmed to body temperature in order to cleanse the bowels.

Begin a course of urine therapy by collecting the first urination of the morning midstream (see Appendix I) and then again late in the afternoon or early evening. The frequency of urine drinking should be slowly increased until every urination passed is drunk.

Urine should be supplemented with distilled water up to a total liquid intake of four litres daily.

Night time urinations should be saved for urine massages.

A complete fast should be observed for between seven and thirty days. During this time only urine and distilled water should be given to drink, and **absolutely no food whatsoever**.

Rest, rest, rest.

Thought pattern reprogramming:

"This moment is filled with joy. I now choose to experience the sweetness of today."

Eczema

Thought pattern trigger:

Breath-taking antagonism. Mental eruptions.

Emotional response:

Annoyance, alienation.

Physical Healing

Perform an enema containing about a half litre of fresh or aged urine warmed to body temperature in order to cleanse the bowels.

Begin a course of urine therapy by collecting the first urination of the morning midstream (see Appendix I) and then again late in the afternoon or early evening, the frequency of urine drinking should be slowly increased until every urination passed is drunk.

Urine should be supplemented with distilled water up to a total liquid intake of four litres daily.

Night time urinations should be saved for urine massages.

Depending on the severity of the symptoms a complete fast should be observed for between three and thirty days. During this time only urine and distilled water should be given to drink, and **absolutely no food whatsoever**.

Thought pattern reprogramming:

"Harmony and peace, love and joy surround me and dwell in me. I am safe and secure."

Emphysema

Thought pattern trigger:

Fear of taking in life. Not worthy of living.

Emotional response:

Fear, hopelessness.

Physical Healing

Begin a course of urine therapy by collecting the first urination of the morning midstream (**see Appendix I**) and then again late in the afternoon or early evening, the frequency of urine drinking should be slowly increased until every urination passed is drunk.

When the stage is reached when all urine passed is drunk, then fast on urine and distilled water eating **no food whatsoever** for 2 - 4 weeks.

Break the fast by eating one or two small meals daily of fresh juicy fruits, berries, nuts and seeds or light leafy green salads (raw salads with no dressing and avoiding fibrous "earthy" vegetables) while continuing to consume urine twice a day and distilled water as required.

Thought pattern reprogramming:

"It is my birthright to live fully and freely. I love life. I love me."

Epilepsy

Thought pattern trigger:

Sense of persecution. Rejection of life. A feeling of great struggle. Self-violence.

Emotional response:

Defensive.

Physical Healing

To stop an epileptic seizure place 10 drops of urine under the tongue of the epileptic (Please note: in such an emergency it need not be the patient's own urine). The seizure should stop within 30 seconds to a minute.

Begin a course of urine therapy by collecting the first urination of the morning midstream (**see Appendix I**) and then again late in the afternoon or early evening, the frequency of urine drinking should be slowly increased until every urination passed is drunk.

When the stage is reached when all urine passed is drunk, then fast on urine and distilled water, eating **no food whatsoever**, for 2 - 4 weeks.

Thought pattern reprogramming:

"I choose to see life as eternal and joyous. I am eternal and joyous and at peace."

Fat

Thought pattern trigger:

Oversensitivity. A need for protection. A resistance to forgive.

Emotional response:

Fear, defensiveness, anger, resentment.

Physical Healing

Begin urine therapy. Drink the first midstream urination of the morning within fifteen minutes of collection, saving a little of the urine to massage into the body, paying particular attention to any area that have become symptomatic. Repeat the process in the late afternoon or early evening. (**see Appendix I**)

Drink distilled water to bring the combined water and urine intake to approximately four litres per day. (**see Appendix II**)

Observe a fast on urine and distilled water eating **no food whatsoever** for 2 - 4 weeks.

Break the fast by eating one or two small meals daily of fresh juicy fruits, berries, nuts and seeds or light leafy green salads (raw salads with no dressing and avoiding fibrous "earthy" vegetables) while continuing to consume urine twice a day and distilled water as required, and continuing to fast two days a week.

Thought pattern reprogramming:

"I am protected by Divine Love. I am always safe and secure. I am willing to grow up and take responsibility for my life. I forgive others, and I now create my own life the way I want it. I am safe"

Fibroid Tumours & Cysts

Thought pattern trigger:

Nursing a hurt from a partner. A blow to the feminine ego.

Emotional response:

Hurt, low self esteem

Physical Healing

Begin urine therapy. Drink the first midstream urination of the morning within fifteen minutes of collection, saving a little of the urine to massage into the body, paying particular attention to any area that have become symptomatic. Repeat the process in the late afternoon or early evening. (**see Appendix I**)

Drink distilled water to bring the combined water and urine intake to approximately four litres per day. (**see Appendix II**)

Observe a fast on urine and distilled water eating **no food whatsoever** for 2 - 4 weeks.

Apply a urine pack to any tumours or cysts. Saturate a clean cotton pad or a clean folded cloth with preferably aged urine, place on the affected area and secure in place with cling film or a gauze, keep wet with additional applications of urine. (**see Appendix I**)

Thought pattern reprogramming:

"I release the pattern in me that attracted this experience. I create only good in my life."

Fibromyalgia

Thought pattern trigger:

Lack of love for what one does. Guilt always seeks punishment.

Emotional response:

Guilt, boredom.

Physical Healing

Begin urine therapy by collecting the first urination of the morning midstream and drink within fifteen minutes of collection. Save a little of the urine to massage into the body. Repeat the process in the late afternoon or early evening. (**see Appendix I**)

Drink distilled water to bring the combined water and urine intake to approximately four litres per day. (**see Appendix II**)

If symptoms of irritable bowel syndrome are experienced then perform an enema containing about a half litre of fresh or aged urine warmed to body temperature once a day for three to five days.

Change diet to small infrequent meals of juicy fruits, nuts or light leafy greens and fast two days per week, these need not be consecutive days. Completely avoid sugar, meat, dairy products, bread, cakes, biscuits and other processed foods. Drink only urine and distilled water.

Thought pattern reprogramming:

"I lovingly release the past. They are free and I am free. All is well in my heart now."

Gangrene

Thought pattern trigger:

Mental morbidity. Drowning of joy with poisonous thoughts.

Emotional response:

Anger, depression.

Physical Healing

Wash the affected area with fresh or aged urine.

Begin a urine fast, which should be observed for between fourteen and thirty days. During this time only urine and distilled water should be given to drink, and **absolutely no food whatsoever**.

Perform regular urine massages three to four times daily and apply a urine pack to the affected area. Saturate a clean cotton pad or a clean folded cloth with aged urine, place on the affected area and secure in place with cling film or gauze, keep wet with additional applications of aged urine.

Thought pattern reprogramming:

"I now choose harmonious thoughts and let the joy flow freely through me."

Gout

Thought pattern trigger:

The need to dominate.

Emotional response:

Impatience, anger.

Physical Healing

Begin urine therapy. Drink the first midstream urination of the morning within fifteen minutes of collection, saving a little of the urine to massage into the body, paying particular attention to any area that have become symptomatic. Repeat the process in the late afternoon or early evening. (**see Appendix I**)

Drink distilled water to bring the combined water and urine intake to approximately four litres per day. (**see Appendix II**)

Make up daily footbaths using aged urine and warmed distilled water, and soak the feet for at least 20 minutes, then massage the feet until dry.

Thought pattern reprogramming:

"I am safe and secure. I am at peace with myself and with others."

Heart Problems

Thought pattern trigger:

Long-standing emotional problems. Lack of joy. Hardening of the heart. Belief in strain and stress.

Emotional response:

Stress, anger, joylessness.

Physical Healing

In the case of a heart attack, place half an ounce of urine under the patient's tongue (Please note: in such an emergency it need not be the patient's own urine).

Change diet to one daily meal of juicy fruits, nuts or light leafy greens and fast two days per week, these need not be consecutive days. Completely avoid sugar, meat, dairy products, bread, cakes, biscuits and other processed foods.

Begin urine therapy. Drink the first midstream urination of the morning within fifteen minutes of collection, saving some of the urine to massage into the body.

Perform urine massages as often as possible paying particular attention to the face, neck and feet. Drink urine again in the late afternoon or early evening. (**see Appendix I**)

Also drink distilled water to bring the combined water and urine intake to approximately four litres per day. (**see Appendix II**)

Thought pattern reprogramming:

"Joy. joy. joy. I lovingly allow joy to flow through· my mind and body and experience."

Hepatitis

Thought pattern trigger:

Resistance to change. Deep seated anger.

Emotional response:

Fear, anger, rage, hatred.

Physical Healing

Perform urine enemas using about a half litre of fresh or aged urine warmed to body temperature, once a day for three to five days.

Begin a course of urine therapy by collecting the first urination of the morning midstream (**see Appendix I**) and then again late in the afternoon or early evening, the frequency of urine drinking should be slowly increased until every urination passed is drunk. Night time urinations should be saved for urine massages.

Urine should be supplemented with distilled water up to a total liquid intake of four litres daily.

Once the stage is reached where every urination is drunk, a complete fast should be observed for between ten and thirty days. During this time only urine and distilled water should be consumed and **absolutely no food whatsoever**.

Thought pattern reprogramming:

"My mind is cleansed and free. I leave the past and move into the new. All is well."

Herpes

Thought pattern trigger:

The need for punishment. Public shame. Belief in a punishing God. Rejection of the genitals.

Emotional response:

Sexual guilt, shame.

Physical Healing

Perform an enema containing about a half litre of fresh or aged urine warmed to body temperature in order to cleanse the bowels.

Begin a course of urine therapy by collecting the first urination of the morning midstream (**see Appendix I**) and then again late in the afternoon or early evening. The frequency of urine drinking should be slowly increased until every urination passed is drunk. Night time urinations should be saved for urine massages.

Urine should be supplemented with distilled water up to a total liquid intake of four litres daily.

Depending on the severity of the symptoms a complete fast should be observed for between three and thirty days. During this time only urine and distilled water should be given to drink, and **absolutely no food whatsoever**.

Rest, rest, rest.

Thought pattern reprogramming:

"My concept of God supports me. I am normal and natural. I rejoice in my own sexuality and in my own body. I am wonderful."

Hodgkin's Disease

Thought pattern trigger:

Blame and a tremendous fear of not being good enough. A frantic race to prove one's self until the blood has no substance left to support itself. The joy of life is forgotten in the race for acceptance.

Emotional response:

Fear, desperation.

Physical Healing

Begin urine therapy. Drink the first midstream urination of the morning within fifteen minutes of collection, saving a little of the urine to massage into the body, Repeat the process in the late afternoon or early evening. (**see Appendix I**)

Urine should be supplemented with distilled water up to a total liquid intake of four litres daily.

Perform regular urine massages three to four times daily, paying particular attention to any swellings in the neck, armpit or groin areas.

Apply a urine packs to the lymph nodes in the neck, armpit or groin, if swollen. Saturate a clean cotton pad or a clean folded cloth with aged urine, place on the affected area and secure in place with cling film or gauze, keep wet with additional applications of aged urine.

Begin a urine fast, which should be observed for between fourteen and thirty days, during this time only urine and distilled water should be given to drink, and **absolutely no food whatsoever**.

Thought pattern reprogramming:

"I am perfectly happy to be me. I am good enough just as I am. I love and approve of myself. I am joy expressing and receiving."

Inflammation

Thought pattern trigger:

Seeing red. Inflamed thinking.

Emotional response:

Fear.

Physical Healing

Begin urine therapy. Drink the first midstream urination of the morning within fifteen minutes of collection. Drink urine again in the late afternoon or early evening. (**see Appendix I**).

Perform urine massages as often as possible paying particular attention to the inflamed areas.

Apply urine packs to the affected areas. Saturate a clean cotton pad or a clean folded cloth with, preferably aged, urine, place on the inflamed area and secure in place with cling film or gauze, keep wet with additional applications of urine as necessary.

Thought pattern reprogramming:

"My thinking is peaceful, calm, and centred."

Influenza

Thought pattern trigger:

Response to mass negativity and beliefs.

Emotional response:

Fear.

Physical Healing

Get plenty of fresh air and sleep with windows open or in a well ventilated room.

Begin urine therapy. Drink the first midstream urination of the morning within fifteen minutes of collection. Repeat the process as often as possible until the late afternoon or early evening. (**see Appendix I**)

Perform at least one urine massage a day, paying particular attention to the face, neck and feet.

If symptoms of sore throat and runny or stuffy nose are experienced then use fresh urine to sniff into the nostrils and gargle until the symptoms abate.

Begin a urine fast, which should be observed for between three and eight days. During this time only urine and distilled water should be given to drink, and **absolutely no food whatsoever**.

Thought pattern reprogramming:

"I am beyond group beliefs. I am free from all congestion and influence."

Kidney Problems

Thought pattern trigger:

Criticism. Failure. Reacting like a little kid.

Emotional response:

Fear, shame, disappointment.

Physical Healing

Begin urine therapy. Drink the first midstream urination of the morning within fifteen minutes of collection, saving a little of the urine to massage into the body, Repeat the process in the late afternoon or early evening. (**see Appendix I**)

If the patient cannot produce any of their own urine then urine from another, preferably a relative of the same sex, may be used instead until the patient is able to pass their own.

If possible, urine should be supplemented with distilled water up to a total liquid intake of four litres daily.

As soon as the patient is consuming their own urine then begin a urine fast, which should be observed for between fourteen and thirty days, during this time only urine and distilled water should be given to drink, and **absolutely no food whatsoever**.

Thought pattern reprogramming:

"Divine right action is always taking place in my life. Only good comes from each experience. It is safe to grow up."

Laryngitis

Thought pattern trigger:

So mad you can't speak. Fear of speaking up. Resentment of authority.

Emotional response:

Fear, resentment.

Physical Healing

Collect the first urination of the morning midstream and use around 2 – 3 tablespoonfuls to gargle with. Repeat 3 – 4 times a day.

Optionally, begin urine therapy. Drink the first urination of the morning within fifteen minutes of collection, saving a little of the urine to massage into the face and neck, Drink again in the late afternoon or early evening. (**see Appendix I**)

Thought pattern reprogramming:

"I am free to ask for what I want. It is safe to express myself I am at peace."

Liver Problems

Thought pattern trigger:

Chronic complaining. Justifying fault-finding to deceive yourself. Feeling bad.

Emotional response:

Anger.

Physical Healing

Begin urine therapy. Drink the first midstream urination of the morning within fifteen minutes of collection. Repeat the process as often as possible until the late afternoon or early evening. (**see Appendix I**)

Perform at least one urine massage a day, paying particular attention to the face, neck and feet.

Urine should be supplemented with distilled water up to a total liquid intake of four litres daily.

Begin a urine fast, which should be observed for ten days. During this time only urine and distilled water should be given to drink, and **absolutely no food whatsoever**.

Thought pattern reprogramming:

"I choose to live through the open space in my heart. I look for love and find it everywhere."

Lung Problems

Thought pattern trigger:

Fear of taking in life. Not feeling worthy of living life fully.

Emotional response:

Depression, grief, fear.

Physical Healing

Get plenty of fresh air and sleep with windows open or in a well ventilated room.

Begin urine therapy. Drink the first midstream urination of the morning within fifteen minutes of collection. Repeat the process as often as possible until the late afternoon or early evening. (**see Appendix I**)

Perform at least one urine massage a day, paying particular attention to the face, neck and feet.

If symptoms of sore throat and runny or stuffy nose are experienced then use fresh urine to sniff into the nostrils and gargle until the symptoms abate.

Begin a urine fast, which should be observed for between three and eight days. During this time only urine and distilled water should be given to drink, and **absolutely no food whatsoever**.

Thought pattern reprogramming:

"I have the capacity to take in the fullness of life. I lovingly live life to the fullest."

Malaria

Thought pattern trigger:

Out of balance with nature and with life.

Emotional response:

Disorientation.

Physical Healing

Begin urine therapy. Drink the first midstream urination of the morning within fifteen minutes of collection. Repeat the process as often as possible until the late afternoon or early evening. (**see Appendix I**)

Perform at least one urine massage a day, paying particular attention to the face, neck and feet.

Urine should be supplemented with distilled water up to a total liquid intake of four litres daily.

Begin a urine fast, which should be observed for ten days, during this time only urine and distilled water should be given to drink, and **absolutely no food whatsoever**.

Thought pattern reprogramming:

"I am united and balanced with all of life. I am safe."

Migraine

Thought pattern trigger:

Dislike of being driven. Resisting the flow of life. Sexual fears.

Emotional response:

Fear.

Physical Healing

Begin urine therapy. Drink the first midstream urination of the morning within fifteen minutes of collection. Repeat the process as often as possible until the late afternoon or early evening. (**see Appendix I**)

Perform at least one urine massage a day, paying particular attention to the face, temples and neck.

Urine should be supplemented with Distilled water up to a total liquid intake of four litres daily.

Begin a urine fast, which should be observed for ten days. During this time only urine and distilled water should be given to drink, and **absolutely no food whatsoever**.

Thought pattern reprogramming:

"I relax into the flow of life and let life provide all that I need easily and comfortably. Life is for me."

Multiple Sclerosis

Thought pattern trigger:

Mental hardness, hard-heartedness, iron will, inflexibility.

Emotional response:

Fear.

Physical Healing

Begin urine therapy. Drink the first midstream urination of the morning within fifteen minutes of collection. Repeat the process as often as possible until the late afternoon or early evening. (**see Appendix I**)

Perform around 3 – 4 urine massages a day, paying particular attention to the face, neck and feet.

Urine should be supplemented with distilled water up to a total liquid intake of four litres daily.

Begin a urine fast, which should be observed for ten days. During this time only urine and distilled water should be given to drink, and **absolutely no food whatsoever**.

Thought pattern reprogramming:

"By choosing loving, joyous thoughts, I create a loving, joyous world. I am safe and free."

Muscular Dystrophy

Thought pattern trigger:

"It's not worth growing up."

Emotional response:

Despair, denial.

Physical Healing

Begin urine therapy. Drink the first midstream urination of the morning within fifteen minutes of collection. Repeat the process as often as possible until the late afternoon or early evening. (**see Appendix I**)

Perform around 3 – 4 urine massages a day, paying particular attention to the face, neck and feet.

Urine should be supplemented with distilled water up to a total liquid intake of four litres daily.

Begin a urine fast, which should be observed for between ten and thirty days. During this time only urine and distilled water should be given to drink, and **absolutely no food whatsoever**.

Thought pattern reprogramming:

"I go beyond my parents' limitations. I am free to be the best me I can."

Osteoporosis

Thought pattern trigger:

"Feeling there is no support left in life."

Emotional response:

Helplessness.

Physical Healing

Begin urine therapy. Drink the first midstream urination of the morning within fifteen minutes of collection. Repeat the process as often as possible until the late afternoon or early evening. (**see Appendix I**)

Perform around 3 – 4 urine massages a day, paying particular attention to the face, neck and feet.

Urine should be supplemented with distilled water up to a total liquid intake of four litres daily.

Begin a urine fast, which should be observed for between fourteen to thirty days. During this time only urine and distilled water should be given to drink, and **absolutely no food whatsoever**.

Thought pattern reprogramming:

"I stand up for myself, and life supports me in unexpected, loving ways."

Parasites

Thought pattern trigger:

Giving power to others, letting them take over.

Emotional response:

Self doubt, helplessness, fear.

Physical Healing

Begin urine therapy. Drink the first midstream urination of the morning within fifteen minutes of collection. Repeat the process as often as possible until the late afternoon or early evening. (**see Appendix I**)

Perform around 3 – 4 urine massages a day, paying particular attention to the face, neck and feet.

Urine should be supplemented with distilled water up to a total liquid intake of four litres daily.

Begin a urine fast, which should be observed for between ten to thirty days. During this time only urine and distilled water should be given to drink, and **absolutely no food whatsoever**.

Break the fast by eating one or two small meals daily of fresh juicy fruits, berries, nuts and seeds or light leafy green salads (raw salads with no dressing and avoiding fibrous "earthy" vegetables) while continuing to consume urine twice a day and distilled water as required.

For stubborn amoebas and tapeworms, collect urine and leave in a glass covered with a paper towel or a cloth, for 12 – 15 hours. Using a second, clean, glass pour the urine from one to the other for a few minutes until the Ammonia evaporates off and the pungent smell subsides then drink. Beware, the detox reaction is likely to be fast and furious, many have reported that, within 10 minutes of drinking their own fermented urine, they experienced severe diarrhoea. This is not a problem however, as long as hydration is maintained with fresh urine and distilled water.

The fermented urine of a person with parasites is so effective that it even removes the parasites' eggs.

Thought pattern reprogramming:

"I lovingly take back my power and eliminate all interference."

Parkinson's Disease

Thought pattern trigger:

Fear and an intense desire to control everything and everyone.

Emotional response:

Fear.

Physical Healing

Begin urine therapy. Drink the first midstream urination of the morning within fifteen minutes of collection. Repeat the process as often as possible until the late afternoon or early evening. (**see Appendix I**)

Perform around 3 – 4 urine massages a day, paying particular attention to the face, neck and feet.

Urine should be supplemented with distilled water up to a total liquid intake of four litres daily.

Begin a urine fast, which should be observed for between ten to thirty days, during this time only urine and distilled water should be given to drink, and **absolutely no food whatsoever**, until symptoms abate.

Break the fast by eating one or two small meals daily of fresh juicy fruits, berries, nuts and seeds or light leafy green salads (raw salads with no dressing and avoiding fibrous "earthy" vegetables) while continuing to consume urine twice a day and distilled water as required.

Thought pattern reprogramming:

"I relax knowing that I am safe. Life is for me, and I trust the process of life."

Psoriasis

Thought pattern trigger:

Fear of being hurt. Refusing to accept responsibility for our own feelings.

Emotional response:

Fear, Denial.

Physical Healing

Perform an enema containing about a half litre of fresh or aged urine warmed to body temperature in order to cleanse the bowels.

Begin a course of urine therapy by collecting the first urination of the morning midstream (**see Appendix I**) and then again late in the afternoon or early evening. The frequency of urine drinking should be slowly increased until every urination passed is drunk.

Pour a small amount of either fresh or aged urine into the palm of the hand and massage it lightly into the affected areas, making sure that the area is well saturated. Continue to massage until the urine has completely absorbed into the skin. Reapply as many times as desired, the more the area is treated in this way the better.

If the skin eruption is severe then use a urine pack. Saturate a clean cotton pad with aged urine, place on the affected areas and secure in place with cling film or a gauze, keep wet with additional applications of aged urine.

Urine should be supplemented with distilled water up to a total liquid intake of four litres daily.

Depending on the severity of the symptoms, a complete fast should be observed for between three and thirty days. During this time only urine and distilled water should be given to drink, and **absolutely no food whatsoever**.

Rest, rest, rest.

Thought pattern reprogramming:

"I am alive to the joys of living. I deserve and accept the very best in life. I love and approve of myself."

Sciatica

Thought pattern trigger:

Being hypocritical. Fear of money and of the future.

Emotional response:

Fear, worry.

Physical Healing

Begin urine therapy by collecting the first urination of the morning midstream and drink within fifteen minutes of collection. Save a little of the urine to massage into the body. Repeat the process in the late afternoon or early evening. (**see Appendix I**)

Place a urine pack over any painful areas, secure in place with cling film and keep wet with regular applications of urine until the acute symptoms subside.

Drink distilled water to bring the combined water and urine intake to approximately four litres per day. (**see Appendix II**)

Observe a complete fast for between three and thirty days. During this time only urine and distilled water should be given to drink, and **absolutely no food whatsoever**.

Thought pattern reprogramming:

"I move into my greater good. My good is everywhere, and I am secure and safe."

Shingles

Thought pattern trigger:

Waiting for the other shoe to drop. Too sensitive.

Emotional response:

Fear, tension.

Physical Healing

Begin urine therapy by collecting the first urination of the morning midstream and drink within fifteen minutes of collection. Save some of the urine to massage into the body. Repeat the process in the late afternoon or early evening. (**see Appendix I**)

Place a urine pack over any painful areas, secure in place with cling film and keep wet with regular applications of urine until the acute symptoms subside.

Pour a small amount of either fresh or aged urine into the palm of the hand and massage it lightly into the affected areas, making sure that the area is well saturated. Continue to massage until the urine has completely absorbed into the skin. Reapply as many times as desired, the more the area is treated in this way the better.

If the skin eruption is severe then use a urine pack. Saturate a clean cotton pad with aged urine, place on the affected areas and secure in place with cling film or a gauze, keep wet with additional applications of aged urine.

Drink distilled water to bring the combined water and urine intake to approximately four litres per day. (**see Appendix II**)

Depending on the severity of the symptoms a complete fast should be observed for between seven and fourteen days. During this time only urine and distilled water should be given to drink, and **absolutely no food whatsoever**.

Thought pattern reprogramming:

"I am relaxed and peaceful because I trust the process of life. All is well in my world."

195

Stomach Problems

Thought pattern trigger:

Fear of the new. Inability to assimilate the new."

Emotional response:

Fear, dread.

Physical Healing

Begin urine therapy by collecting the first urination of the morning midstream and drink within fifteen minutes of collection, save a little of the urine to massage into the body. Repeat the process in the late afternoon or early evening. (**see Appendix I**)

Drink distilled water to bring the combined water and urine intake to approximately four litres per day. (**see Appendix II**)

Thought pattern reprogramming:

"Life agrees with me. I assimilate the new every moment of every day. All is well."

Thrush

Thought pattern trigger:

Anger over making the wrong decisions.

Emotional response:

Anger, regret.

Physical Healing

Wash the vagina and vulva thoroughly with fresh urine 2 – 3 times a day.

Begin urine therapy by collecting the first urination of the morning midstream and drink within fifteen minutes of collection. Repeat the process in the late afternoon or early evening. (**see Appendix I**)

If there is pain, apply a urine pack. Saturate a clean cotton pad with, preferably aged, urine and place on the affected areas and secure in place with cling film or a gauze, keep wet with additional applications of urine.

Thought pattern reprogramming:

"I lovingly accept my decisions, knowing I am free to change. I am safe."

Thyroid Problems

Thought pattern trigger:

"I never get to do what I want to do. When is it going to be my turn?"

Emotional response:

Humiliation.

Physical Healing

Begin a course of urine therapy by collecting the first urination of the morning midstream (see Appendix I) and then again late in the afternoon or early evening. Gradually increase frequency of urine drinking until every urination passed is drunk.

Pour a small amount of either fresh or aged urine into the palm of the hand and massage it lightly into the entire body, paying particular attention to the face, neck and feet. Massage the urine into the skin until it has completely absorbed. Apply 1 – 2 times daily.

Urine should be supplemented with distilled water up to a total liquid intake of four litres daily.

Depending on the severity of the symptoms a complete fast should be observed for between five and fourteen days. During this time only urine and distilled water should be given to drink, and **absolutely no food whatsoever**.

Thought pattern reprogramming:

"I move beyond old limitations and now allow myself to express freely and creatively."

Tonsillitis

Thought pattern trigger:

Repressed emotions. Stifled creativity.

Emotional response:

Fear.

Physical Healing

Begin urine therapy. Drink the first urination of the morning within fifteen minutes of collection, drink again in the late afternoon or early evening. (**see Appendix I**)

Use around 2 – 3 tablespoonfuls of the collected urine to gargle with. Repeat 3 – 4 times a day.

Pour a small amount of either fresh or aged urine into the palm of the hand and massage it lightly into the face and neck, making sure that the area is well saturated, and continue to massage until the urine has completely absorbed into the skin. Reapply as many times as desired, the more the area is treated in this way the better.

If symptoms persist for more than 3 days, continue as above and fast for three to five days. During this time only urine and distilled water should be given to drink, and **absolutely no food whatsoever**.

Thought pattern reprogramming:

"My good now flows freely. Divine ideas express through me. I am at peace."

Tuberculosis

Thought pattern trigger:

Wasting away from selfishness. Possessive. Cruel thoughts. Revenge.

Emotional response:

Anger.

Physical Healing

Perform an enema containing about a half litre of fresh or aged urine warmed to body temperature in order to cleanse the bowels.

Begin a course of urine therapy by collecting the first urination of the morning midstream (see Appendix I) and then again late in the afternoon or early evening. The frequency of urine drinking should be slowly increased until every urination passed is drunk.

Urine should be supplemented with distilled water up to a total liquid intake of four litres daily.

Night time urinations should be saved for urine massages.

Depending on the severity of the symptoms a complete fast should be observed for between three and thirty days. During this time only urine and distilled water should be given to drink, and **absolutely no food whatsoever**.

Rest, rest, rest.

Thought pattern reprogramming:

"As I love and approve of myself, I create a joyful, peaceful world to live in."

Varicose Veins

Thought pattern trigger:

Standing in a hateful situation. Feeling overworked and overburdened.

Emotional response:

Discouragement.

Physical Healing

Begin urine therapy by collecting the first urination of the morning midstream and drink within fifteen minutes of collection. Repeat the process in the late afternoon or early evening. (**see Appendix I**)

Pour a small amount of either fresh or aged urine into the palm of the hand and massage it lightly into the affected area, making sure that the area is well saturated. Continue to massage until the urine has completely absorbed into the skin. Reapply as many times as desired, the more the area is treated in this way the better.

If the veins are especially pronounced, or they are painful, apply a urine pack. Saturate a clean cotton pad with, preferably aged, urine and place on the affected areas and secure in place with cling film or a gauze, keep wet with additional applications of urine.

Thought pattern reprogramming:

"I stand in truth and live and move in joy. I love Life, and circulate freely."

Venereal Disease

Thought pattern trigger:

Need for punishment. Belief that the genitals are sinful or dirty. Abusing another.

Emotional response:

Sexual guilt.

Physical Healing

Begin urine therapy by collecting the first urination of the morning midstream and drink within fifteen minutes of collection. Repeat the process in the late afternoon or early evening. (**see Appendix I**)

Pour a small amount of either fresh or aged urine into the palm of the hand and massage it lightly into any affected areas, making sure that the area is well saturated. Continue to massage until the urine has completely absorbed into the skin. Reapply as many times as desired, the more the area is treated in this way the better.

If symptoms persist for more than 3 days, continue as above and fast for five to seven days, during this time only urine and distilled water should be given to drink, and **absolutely no food whatsoever**.

Thought pattern reprogramming:

"I lovingly and joyously accept my sexuality and its expression. I accept only thoughts that support me and make me feel good."

"For fuck's sake, stand up and save yourself."

Allegedly K. A. Dave.

Appendix I

Urine Therapy

Fresh Urine

Freshly collected urine is considered perfectly sterile and totally safe for internal ingestion. However, it begins to break down on contact with the air and the bacteria in the air cause ammonia to form in the urine.

Fresh urine must be used within 12 to 15 minutes of collection, after which the formation of ammonia causes the urine to take on an overpowering odour. However, urine therapy practitioners who have collected urine in the early hours of the morning have reported that the ammonia can be evaporated off by pouring the urine from one container to another for a few minutes before drinking.

Regardless, it is not recommended to orally use urine more than 15 minutes after collection.

Aged Urine

Aged urine is more effective for external uses. Between about 4 - 8 days the urine begins to ferment and develop a very pungent odour, which seems to be extremely beneficial in treating skin conditions. However, urine can be aged indefinitely and it appears that its effects improve with time.

To age urine, collect it in a dark bottle stopped with a wad of cotton wool, to allow the urine to breathe (fortunately the powerful smell does not seem to escape) and store the bottle in a cool dark place.

It should be stressed that aged urine is for **external uses only**.

How to perform urine therapy

1. Clean the genital area with a little soap and water before collecting urine.
2. In a clean glass, collect the first urination of the morning midstream, that is, discard the first and last 5 - 10 ml.
3. Separate and set aside a small amount of the collected urine for later use.

4. Drink the urine within fifteen minutes of collection – There are many ways to take urine orally including:
   - Using a dropper bottle, one or two drops can be placed under the tongue and the dosage can be increased to five to ten drops twice a day over a period of three to five days until one becomes accustomed to the taste.
   - Urine can be mixed with freshly squeezed fruit juice.
   - Urine can be drunk neat while holding the breath and while still holding the breath and few mouthfuls of distilled water or freshly squeezed fruit juice can be taken to rinse the palate of any taste.
   - Or just drink it neat and stop being a pussy.
5. Use some of the urine set aside earlier to wash the body. Pour a little into the palm of the hand and massage into a section of the body at a time until it completely absorbs into the skin.
6. Repeat this procedure in the late afternoon/early evening.

Urine Fasting

Fasting on urine is a very powerful curative practice; it cleanses the blood by stimulating the liver, lungs and skin to remove toxins.

Simply drink all the urine you pass along with as much distilled water as required throughout the day; the urine will quickly change to an almost neutral, slightly saline taste and results become apparent very quickly indeed.

It is advised that urine is not drunk in the evening, as one of its effects is a sudden burst of energy that often makes it difficult to get to sleep.

Homeopathic preparation

A homeopathic preparation can be formulated during the onset of an illness. At that time the urine contains specific antibodies, antigens and immune defence agents for the particular illness.

The homeopathic preparation provides a means of preserving the collected urine for use whenever the illness strikes.

1. Clean the genital area with a little soap and water prior to urine collection.
2. Collect midstream urine in a clean glass.
3. Add one drop of the fresh urine to 5ml of distilled water in a sterile bottle, seal and shake 50 times.

4. Take one drop of this mix and add to another 5ml ounce of distilled water and shake 50 times.
5. Take one drop of this mix and add to 5ml. of 80 to 90 proof vodka as a preservative.

Use this solution by placing three drops under the tongue hourly until there is obvious improvement or a temporary worsening of symptoms.   As improvement progresses, increase the interval between treatments.

After three days, suspend treatment to avoid over taxing the immune system. However if there is no further improvement or a relapse then resume treatment.

Urine Packs

A urine pack is a urine compress that work extremely effectively with skin disorders such as swelling and redness, cuts, bruises, burns, boils, eczema, psoriasis, athlete's foot, ringworm, poison ivy, ulcers and tumours or any type of abnormal growth on the skin.

Urine packs are also useful in infusing urine's beneficial substances into the tissues beneath the skin.

1. Soak a gauze, a cotton wool ball or a cloth with preferably aged urine, although fresh urine can also be used.
2. Place the urine pack over the site of the injury and hold it in place by wrapping it with cling film and optionally tie in place with gauze strips.
3. Keep the dressing wet with additional applications of urine every few hours.
4. Urine packs should be in combination with internal urine

Urine Massages

Urine can be applied to the skin using either fresh or aged urine.   Aged urine is generally more effective, but it has a pungent odour.

Small amounts of urine can be poured into the palm of the hand and massaged into one section of the body at a time until it completely absorbs into the skin. Once absorbed the urine does not smell so you can leave it on the skin or rinse it off after an hour or so.

The urine acts as a moisturiser, a natural soap, an after shave lotion, it returns the softness and elasticity to the skin, it also stimulates the skin to eliminate toxins and so is very effective with all kinds of skin problems such as itching, sunburns, eczema, psoriasis and acne. When massaged into the hair and scalp it cleans and softens the hair and often stimulates new hair growth.

Massaging the whole body is an important complement to both drinking urine and fasting as it provides many valuable substances to the body through the skin.

Other uses

- For eye strain, conjunctivitis, red or tired eyes, use an eyewash cup and bathe the eyes in urine, blinking fifty times and perhaps perform eye exercises.
- For ear problems, pour a little urine into the ears and stopper the ears with cotton balls dipped in coconut oil to prevent leakage.
- For sinus problems, sniff urine into the nostrils.
- For throat problems or toothache, gargle with urine.
- For any skin or nail problems on the feet such as athlete's foot or ringworm, put aged urine in a footbath with warm water and soak the feet for 20 minutes then massage the feet until dry.
- For colon, stomach or digestive problems, warm some fresh (or aged) urine to body temperature and cleanse the colon by performing a urine enema.
- Urine can be used as a vaginal douche, useful in cases such as yeast problems, white discharge, etc.

Detoxification Symptoms

A common occurrence during the initial stages of urine therapy is what is known as detoxification symptoms or a healing crisis. As stored toxins are released and removed from the body, symptoms such as headache, nausea, diarrhoea, tiredness, or skin rashes may appear, and it is also likely that the symptoms that urine therapy is being taken to address will flare up and so seem counterproductive.

These symptoms can seem to be intense, however, they tend to disappear over the course of one to three days. Some urine therapy practitioners will suggest that the dosage of urine should be backed down when detox symptoms are encountered until the reactions subside but since we know that symptoms are actually beneficial indications of the body's healing status. It is better to step up the urine intake to exacerbate the body's cleansing.

Appendix II

Distilled Water

Distilled water is essentially pure H_2O – a bath of negatively charged particles which is important because all waste, debris and inorganic substances lodged within you are positively charged.

Drinking a significant amount of distilled water every day will restore the human body to its perfect state. However, drinking from sources such as tap water, well water, river water, spring water, mineral water or bottled water all contain inorganic minerals and a whole raft of contaminants and cause calcification, hardening of the arteries and organs and a variety of ailments.

Sources of Distilled Water

Natural precipitation, that is, rainwater, mist, snow, dew and fog are the main ways that nature produces distilled water. Unfortunately, due to pollution and chemtrails these natural sources may well need to be further filtered.

The water in juiced fruits and vegetables is also distilled but, once again, with the massive use of chemical fertilisers and pesticides even this liquid may well be tainted unless the fruits and vegetables are grown organically.

The human body also produces distilled water in the form of urine. The human kidney distils the water from the blood by squeezing the blood through tiny channels called nephrons.

The only man made distilled water is produced by the process of steam distillation, that is, boiling water to steam and then condensing the steam to pure water, leaving behind the impurities.

Please note that de-ionised water is not distilled water.

Drinking Distilled Water

For best results it is advised that about four and a half litres of distilled liquids are drunk each day.

1. On awakening drink two glasses.
2. Another two glasses just before breakfast.
3. Two glasses in the middle of the morning.
4. Two more glasses at midday.
5. Two glasses in the middle of the afternoon.
6. Another two glasses late afternoon/early evening.
7. The last two glasses in the evening shortly before going to bed.

Oxygenated Water

In the distant past, rainwater used to be highly oxygenated as the rain clouds would condense high in the atmosphere where the water vapour (H_2O) would interact with the unstable gas Ozone (O_3) and small amounts of Hydrogen Peroxide (H_2O_2) would form. Today, however the pollution in the atmosphere causes rain clouds to condense significantly lower where the water vapour can no longer come into contact with the Ozone.

Distilled water can be oxygenated by the addition of 35% Food Grade Hydrogen Peroxide, but since the body has adapted to much lower levels, the Hydrogen Peroxide must be introduced gradually, starting with 3 drops in an 8 ounce glass of water three times a day and increasing daily until the maintenance dosage is reached. (25 drops)

Day Number	Number of Drops	Number of Times Per Day
1	3	3
2	4	3
3	5	3
4	6	3
5	7	3
6	8	3
7	9	3
8	10	3
9	12	3
10	14	3
11	16	3
12	18	3
13	20	3
14	22	3
15	24	3
16	25	3

Suggested Hydrogen Peroxide dosage protocol

After the maintenance dosage is reached on day 16, the dosage is maintained for a week and then can be gradually tapered off to:

25 drops once a day for a week

25 drops once every other day for two weeks

25 drops once every third day for three weeks

25 drops once every fourth day for four weeks

The effect of adding Hydrogen Peroxide is to flood the body with oxygen. Healthy cells and friendly bacteria are what are known as "aerobic" which means that they thrive in an oxygen rich environment. Cancer cells and most harmful bacteria are anaerobic and cannot survive in an oxygenated environment.

Hydrogen peroxide saturates the cells and tissues with oxygen and stimulates the body's enzymes to clear out toxins. According to Dr. Charles Farr it also:

"...triggers an increase in the metabolic rate, causes small arteries to dilate and increase blood flow, enhances the body's distribution and consumption of oxygen and raises body temperature"

Handling Hydrogen Peroxide

Only 35% **Food Grade** Hydrogen Peroxide can be used internally. However, hydrogen peroxide is a powerful oxidizer and must always be diluted with distilled water; otherwise it can be extremely dangerous or even fatal.

Care must be taken when handling it. If it comes into contact with the skin, rinse with water. The skin will temporarily turn white, but it will not cause any permanent harm.

Hydrogen peroxide will also break down into water and oxygen if placed in direct sunshine, so store it in a tightly sealed container in the freezer.

Hydrogen peroxide has many other beneficial uses at the 3% concentration, such as a body spray after a shower, a mouthwash, a vaginal douche or as an enema. To make a 3% solution, simply mix one part of 35% hydrogen peroxide with eleven parts of distilled water.

Detoxification Symptoms

It is very important that detox symptoms are not confused with the idea that distilled water is causing illness.

Distilled water will dissolve and wash away mineral deposits and toxins but as in all cases of detoxification, toxins that have been ingested and inhaled for a whole lifetime will find a way to be ejected from the body, so there will be detox symptoms but the type and location will depend on the illness.

Detox symptoms may include:

Spots and rashes	*Vomiting*
Diarrhoea	*Headaches*
Flu-like symptoms	*Nausea*
Heavy sweating	*Bad breath*
Smelly armpits	

And just like all symptoms, detox symptoms are good things. They are the temporary indication that the body is engaged in the elimination of toxins.

Further Reading

The Water of Life: A Treatise on Urine Therapy

John W. Armstrong

2005 Random House UK (ISBN: 978-0091906603)

Your Own Perfect Medicine

Martha M. Christie

1996 Wishland (ISBN: 978-0963209115)

Urine Therapy: Nature's Elixir for Good Health

Flora Peschek-Böhmer, Gisela Schreiber

1999 Healing Arts Press (ISBN: 978-0892817993)

You Can Heal Your Life

Louise L. Hay.

1984 Hay House (ISBN: 978-0937611012)

Man's Higher Consciousness

Hilton Hotema

2010 Kessinger Publishing (ISBN: 978-1169830141)

Man, The Unknown

Dr. Alexis Carrel

1967 Harper (ASIN: B0007IX4KI)

Morphic Resonance: The Nature of Formative Causation

Dr. Rupert Sheldrake

2009 Park Street Press (ISBN: 978-1594773174)

Printed in Great Britain
by Amazon

26437201R00119